Praise for *The LO*

"A graceful and beautiful book for those enduring breast cancer treatment. Sharon Brock will hold your hand, soothe your soul, calm your emotions and lift your spirits as you move through your healing and recovery."
—**Katherine Woodward Thomas,** *New York Times* bestselling author of *Calling in "The One"* and *Conscious Uncoupling*

"In this uplifting book, Sharon Brock takes the reader on her intimate breast cancer journey and shows how mindfulness and self-compassion helped her every step of the way. It is a generous book that inspires hope and offers wise companionship to those navigating this difficult terrain. Highly recommended!"
—**Chris Germer,** PhD, bestselling author of *The Mindful Path to Self-Compassion: Freeing Yourself from Destructive Thoughts and Emotions*

"Sharon does an incredible job of weaving together a vulnerable and beautiful personal memoir about her experience with cancer with practical lessons in mindfulness and guided meditations you can use to make it through your own journey with acceptance, compassion, equanimity and love. This book is ideal for anyone recently diagnosed with cancer, as well as anyone coping with a difficult moment in life. Sharon speaks from the heart. She soothes, she inspires, she connects—she is the real deal."
—**MeiMei Fox,** *New York Times* bestselling author of *Bend, Not Break*

"Sharon Brock's heartfelt integrity radiates from every word she writes. Her transmission unlocks the heart of mindfulness. This book is a gift for a loved one with a cancer diagnosis, as well as those who love them. Much to be gleaned. Benefits to be had. Blessings to be received. Beautiful work."
—**Ben Decker,** bestselling author of *Practical Meditation for Beginners and Modern Spirituality*

"In this vulnerable account, Sharon skillfully teaches mindfulness practices through storytelling. She bravely shares her (s)hero's journey in a way that gives us incredible inspiration and practical takeaways. This book gives us the courage to face the unknown and turn obstacles into doorways to deep wisdom and inner peace."

–**Justin Michael Williams,** bestselling author of *Stay Woke: A Meditation Guide for the Rest of Us*

"LOVEE is a simple, easy-to-follow roadmap to cultivate new habits of emotional resilience and wellbeing. Sharon's experience as a breast cancer patient reveals many powerful insights and we all benefit from her willingness to share."

–**Kaia Roman,** bestselling author of *The Joy Plan: How I Took 30 Days to Stop Worrying, Quit Complaining, and Find Ridiculous Happiness*

"The LOVEE Method is not just for people going through a health crisis. As an entrepreneur, this meditation is one of the tools that has helped me to remain even-keeled, calm and balanced. This practice has helped me tap into a deep knowingness to make the tough decisions life requires of us. The LOVEE Method is truly groundbreaking and can help so many people feel more grounded and positive!"

–**Sage Lavine,** bestselling author of *Women Rocking Business*

"Smart, kind, real (and a joy to read) - this honest book will be your best friend and your best guide all in one."

–**Marianne Cantwell,** bestselling author of *Be a Free Range Human: Escape the 9-5, Create a Life you Love and Still Pay the Bills*

THE LOVEE METHOD

Mindfulness Meditation for Breast Cancer

Sharon Brock, M.S.

Copyright © 2022 Sharon Brock, M.S.

All rights reserved. No part of this book may be used or reproduced by any means, graphic, electronic, or mechanical, including photocopying, recording, taping or by any information storage retrieval system without the written permission of the author except in the case of brief quotations embodied in critical articles and reviews.

Because of the dynamic nature of the Internet, any web addresses or links contained in this book may have changed since publication and may no longer be valid. The views expressed in this work are solely those of the author.

The author of this book does not dispense medical advice or prescribe the use of any technique as a form of treatment for physical, emotional, or medical problems without the advice of a physician, either directly or indirectly. The intent of the author is only to offer information of a general nature to help you in your quest for emotional and spiritual wellbeing. In the event you use any of the information in this book for yourself, which is your right, the author assumes no responsibly for your actions.

For every woman who has been touched by breast cancer, this book is from my heart to yours. May this book serve as a source of strength, peace, and comfort in your life.

Contents

Foreword ix
Introduction xi

Part 1   "L" is for Label
Chapter 1   The Phone Call 3
Chapter 2   All the Doctors. 10
Chapter 3   The Label Practice—Label the Emotion 19
The Label Practice Meditation 26

Part 2   "O" is for Observe
Chapter 4   The Difference between Pain and Suffering 31
Chapter 5   Living with Uncertainty 35
Chapter 6   The Observe Practice—Observe the Emotion. 41
The Observe Practice Meditation 47

Part 3   "V" is for Value
Chapter 7   Going into the Fire. 53
Chemotherapy Meditation 62
Chapter 8   I'm Only Human 65

Chapter 9   The Value Practice—Value the Emotion............72
The Value Practice Meditation 80

Part 4   "E" is for Embrace
Chapter 10   All We Need Is Love............................85
Chapter 11   Treat Yourself Like Someone You Love............93
Compassionate Body Scan Meditation 103
Chapter 12   The Embrace Practice—Embrace the Emotion.......108
The Embrace Practice Meditation 117

Part 5   "E" is for Equanimity
Chapter 13   Welcome to Pure Land..........................121
Working with Physical Pain Meditation 130
Chapter 14   Strength Through Surrender....................133
Healing Visualization Meditation 143
Chapter 15   The Equanimity Practice—Accept the Situation...145
The Equanimity Practice Meditation 156

Part 6   Putting LOVEE Altogether
Chapter 16   After Cancer, Challenges Still Arise...........161
Chapter 17   The LOVEE Method—Build Emotional Resilience...171
The LOVEE Method Meditation 179
Chapter 18   Moving Forward with a New Perspective..........182

Acknowledgements..188
Endnotes 190
Additional Resources 193

Foreword

It has been a pleasure to know Sharon Brock as one of my mindfulness students. Sharon graduated from the UCLA Training in Mindfulness Facilitation program in 2019, and I was her primary teacher. During her participation in our 10-month training program, Sharon was also receiving breast cancer treatment at UCLA Medical Center.

It was inspiring to witness Sharon's transformation over the course of the year. Since she was going through such a challenging time, she was an eager mindfulness student, practiced for many hours a day, and therefore experienced the healing wisdom of these practices firsthand.

Even though she was undergoing chemotherapy, she attended every class, made an effort to connect with other students, and contributed insightful ideas to class discussions. I was always impressed by her inquiring mind and thoughtful questions. Every three months, we gathered in person for a retreat and whenever I saw Sharon her hair was a bit shorter, but her awareness was becoming brighter as the year progressed. As she was declining on the outside, she was becoming stronger on the inside due to her consistent mindfulness practice.

Sharon is the perfect person to write this book. Not only does she have a background in neuroscience and medical journalism, she has an uplifting spirit that offers hope and positivity to everyone she meets—and staying hopeful and positive is essential for anyone going through cancer treatment.

This is not simply a "how-to" book. In the memoir chapters, Sharon vulnerably shares how cancer affected every aspect of her life—her finances, her self-esteem, and her relationships. I know these stories will be supportive to readers. I also love the humor sprinkled throughout the book. Sharon succeeds in teaching the five mindfulness practices through storytelling, making the book both instructional and enjoyable to read.

My favorite part of the book is when Sharon's mindfulness practice resulted in having zero side effects after her final chemo session. Her doctors said that side effects were cumulative, so Sharon was expecting the worst. Having no side effects was evidence of the mind-body connection and the healing power of mindfulness.

Throughout my year working with Sharon, I witnessed her trusting that her mindfulness practice would not only help her stay emotionally balanced during her treatments, but also reveal profound insights necessary for emotional healing and growth. These insights are shared with you in this wonderful book.

We all need skills for working with life's challenges right in the moment when we're struggling the most. This makes this book a helpful companion for anyone going through cancer treatment, or even other struggles in life. If we have a daily mindfulness practice while we are going through a difficult time, we can become kinder, happier, and more integrated people. As evidenced by Sharon's story, rather than become pessimistic about life, her dedicated practice helped her to move through this challenge in a powerful way and emerge a stronger and more grateful person—and this book can help readers do the same.

–**Diana Winston,** Director of Mindfulness Education at UCLA MARC, bestselling author of *Fully Present: The Science, Art, and Practice of Mindfulness*

Introduction

*"When we are no longer able to change a situation,
we are challenged to change ourselves."*
Viktor Frankl, Holocaust survivor

The Moment Everything Changed

On April 30, 2018, I got the news that no one ever wants to hear.

"I'm sorry, Sharon. You have cancer," said my doctor over the phone.

Holding the phone to my ear, I sat down at my kitchen table and went into shock. My entire body froze, and my consciousness soared from sea level to thirty-thousand feet. I tried to listen to my doctor's instructions, but I couldn't understand a word. My mind was spinning with panic and disbelief. *What is going on here? Is this really happening? Am I going to die?*

I hung up the phone and stared at the wall. Nothing made sense anymore. I was only forty-four years old, and cancer didn't run in my family. I was a health journalist and a meditation teacher, and I practiced yoga on a daily basis. Being healthy was a big part of my identity. *I was the healer, not the sick person.*

In my life, I'd heard this message over and over again: "If you eat well and exercise, you won't get sick." Yet, here I was, someone with a healthy diet and a daily exercise routine with a life-threatening disease. The very foundation of my understanding of cause-and-effect, and how the world works, was shattered into a million pieces.

The emotion that was front-and-center, however, was the fear of death. It was an alarm that shook my psyche to the core. A feeling of terror that I had never experienced before. I knew that I would die someday, but now I *really* knew, and I feared that my final day might arrive sooner than later.

Although I had experienced a fair amount of difficulties in my life, nothing had prepared me for this. I couldn't just walk away from cancer, like a bad job or flaky boyfriend. It was literally *inside* of me. I couldn't push it away or escape it, so I had to learn a new skill—how to *be* with it. Having cancer would be my reality for months, years, or possibly forever. To cope, I had to create a new consciousness that would allow me to stay still, let go of control, and fully accept the card I'd been dealt. I had to learn how to persevere and move *through* this challenge rather than run from it. The only way out was through.

Tiny Sailboat, Torrential Waves

The emotional experience of having cancer is similar to being alone on a sailboat upon stormy seas. Up until that point, my life's journey had been slightly rocky, with a few ups and downs. But the day I received that dreaded phone call from my doctor, it was as if a massive gust of wind suddenly hit my sail, tipping my boat—and my sanity—to a forty-five-degree angle and catapulting the boat to Mach speed. I held on to the side rails of that sailboat for months, not knowing where I was headed or if the boat would capsize at any moment.

I was hit with my mortality, triggering the highest level of anxiety I had ever experienced. I became laser-focused on finding ways to cope emotionally while traveling on the tumultuous voyage of cancer treatment.

As a meditation teacher, I knew that meditation could help me find some peace. Even though my nervous system was perpetually on high alert, my meditation practice was the ballast that kept me from capsizing. My daily practice kept me even-keeled, hopeful, and even grateful for the good things in my life.

I tried multiple types of meditation. Some worked to reduce my suffering, some didn't. Of all the meditations, I found the mindfulness practices from the Buddhist tradition to be the most effective. To be mindful means to pay attention to our present-moment experience with openness, curiosity, and a willingness to be with what *is*. Mindfulness practices bring our attention from the past or the future into the present moment.

It has been said that necessity is the mother of invention. Due to my desperate need to soothe my anxiety, I spent hours a day working with various mindfulness exercises. I found the most effective practices were labeling and observing my emotions, as well as self-compassion and equanimity. I discovered that when I sat with these practices in this specific order—Label, Observe, Value, Embrace, and Equanimity—I was able to calm the hills and valleys of my emotions and handle this dire circumstance with greater ease and strength.

This process led to organic creation of the LOVEE Method, a five-step mindfulness tool to develop emotional resilience.

Over time, I realized the LOVEE Method was not only helpful for calming my emotions related to health, but it was also a useful tool to process my emotions related to any problematic situation in life. The LOVEE Method helps reduce suffering, regardless of the cause.

The Structure of This Book

This teaching memoir is divided into five parts—one for each letter of the acronym LOVEE, plus a sixth part explaining how the letters work altogether to soothe and process painful emotions. The first two chapters of each part is a memoir and the third chapter teaches a mindfulness practice.

Although mindfulness is secular, its roots stem from Buddhist philosophy and psychology. The third chapter of each part also describes the interconnection between ancient wisdom and modern science, and includes studies from top researchers in the fields of neuroscience and psychology.

It's essential to have first-hand experiences with each meditation. Therefore, I've included meditation scripts throughout the book. **If you'd like to listen to the meditations, recorded audios can be found here:** www.meditationforbreastcancer.com

The best way for you to learn these mindfulness techniques and experience emotional wellbeing on a consistent basis is to take **The LOVEE Method Online Course** along with reading the book.

As a thank you for purchasing the book, I'm offering you a **50% discount** for the course. Simply go to www.meditationforbreastcancer.com/lovee-online-course and enter the **discount code LOVEE50** at checkout.

The Intersection of Science and Spirituality

The goal of this book is not to replace Western medicine with meditation. The purpose is to offer a mindfulness tool to cultivate mental clarity and emotional ease while going through a challenging time, such as a health crisis. When the mind is calm, we can actively participate in the healing of the body along with our physicians and nurses. With the LOVEE Method, the mind can be a part of our healing team.

During my treatments, I discovered the connection between the mind and the body. When my mind was relaxed, my body's immune system was fortified, and I was able to recover from chemotherapy sessions faster. Therefore, I was committed to keeping my mind positive with daily mindfulness practices, for both mental and physical healing.

I believe whole-heartedly that science and spirituality are not mutually exclusive, rather they complement each other. This book honors both Eastern and Western modalities, for comprehensive wellness of the mind, the body, and the Spirit.

Throughout this book, I use the word "Spirit" when referring to an energy that I believe to be divine. I believe that Spirit is *within* all beings, and when we are present and expressing our authentic essence, we are expressing our Spirit. In a gesture of inclusivity, I welcome you to swap out the word Spirit for whatever concept is meaningful for you.

Whatever challenge you are faced with right now, I sincerely hope the LOVEE Method can serve to process your emotions and help you discover the infinite peace that resides within. LOVEE is a powerful tool to address your emotions as they arise, tap into your inner wisdom and compassion, and cultivate a greater sense of ease and confidence as the captain of your sailboat on the stormy seas of life.

Part 1
"L" *is for* **Label**

Chapter 1
The Phone Call

"You can't stop the waves, but you can learn to surf."
Jon Kabat-Zinn, mindfulness teacher

The First Blow

It was the first day of March, and there was a chill in the air. I rolled out of bed like any other day—tired, cranky, and resisting the thought of going to work. My job as a blog editor for a multimillion-dollar fitness company in Los Angeles was fast-paced and stressful. I made a strong cup of coffee, got ready for the day, and drove to work.

As I walked into the office building, I immediately sensed that something was wrong. I arrived at my desk and noticed the silence of the blog team, who were typically cheerful and chatty.

"Hey, what's going on?" I said to my co-worker. She looked at me with a straight face and slightly shook her head.

I sat down at my desk and noticed three lemons next to my computer.

"I brought those in for you," my co-worker said. "I thought they could brighten your day since this could be a tough one for you."

"What?" I said with a perplexed look on my face. Shortly after, my boss walked over to my desk.

"Hey, Sharon," he said. "Could you come to my office?" My stomach dropped, and my heart started racing. I stood up slowly, walked into his office and closed the door.

"I'm sorry, Sharon," he said. "The company has made another budget cut, and you are part of a hundred-person layoff. A third of the company has been let go."

My jaw dropped. This wasn't the perfect job, but it had its perks. My co-workers were great, there was a gym on the second floor, and I taught a meditation class every week.

"Please know that this is not based on your performance," he said. "You've done great work over the years, and we all enjoy working with you."

My head was spinning with emotions ranging from shock to desperation. There were a million things I wanted to say at that moment. But, when I opened my mouth, all I could say was, "Okay, thank you," while looking down at the floor.

By the time I returned to my desk, the technology team had already taken my computer. All that was left were the three lemons.

"Well, here's my farewell dance," I said while juggling the lemons. As the lemons fell to the ground, my co-worker began to laugh. It was her first smile of the day.

"Are you making lemonade out of those lemons?" she asked.

"Ha, well, don't I always?" I said. "I'm trying, at least."

"I'm going to miss you," she said.

"I'll miss you, too," I said and offered her a hug.

By noon, I was in my car driving home.

As I was pacing in my living room, my mind was all over the place. I felt sad about leaving my friends at this job, but also resentful for working hard for so many years just to be laid off. *It's so unfair! I didn't deserve that!*

Being the optimist that I was, I took a deep breath and thought, *Okay, how can I turn this into a good thing? What's the opportunity here?*

For the last three years, I'd been saving money to travel to Spain and walk the Camino, which takes about a month to complete. I'd been so busy with work that I didn't know when I could take that much time off.

The "Camino" is short for *El Camino de Santiago*, or The Way of Saint James. This trek across Spain is an ancient pilgrimage to the tomb of Saint James the Great. Walking the Camino was a life-long dream of mine, and although I hadn't planned on taking this trip for another few months, I realized that now was the time.

The only thing stopping me was money. I had not saved enough money to afford the cost of this trip as well as my rent. And having been laid-off, the date of my next paycheck was uncertain. I knew it was risky, but the only way I could make this work was to move out of my current home, put my stuff into storage, and find a new place to live when I got back.

Why not? I thought, *I'm strong and healthy. I could pull that off. When else will I have four straight weeks to do this? This is the time to go for it!*

I sat down on my couch and called Will, a man I'd been dating for a couple of months. He was charming, intelligent, and kind, and although I didn't know him that well, my feelings for him were already strong.

The only way this trip to Spain could be better was if he joined me. I took a deep breath into that possibility and gave him a call.

"Hey, Sharon, how are you?" Will said as he answered the phone.

"Hey, hon, I'm doing alright," I said. "I have good news and bad news."

"Oh, what happened?" he said. "Bad news first."

"Well, I was laid off from work today," I said, matter-of-factly.

"Oh, no, that's terrible. I'm sorry to hear that," he said. "So, what is the good news?"

"Since I have free time now, I've decided to go to Spain and walk the Camino," I said.

"Oh, nice! You're going to do that trek," he said. "I know you've wanted to do it for a long time."

"Yeah, I'm really excited about it," I said. I paused and took another deep breath. "So … do you want to join me?"

I knew this question was risky. Although Will worked from home and would be able to take the trip logistically and financially, he had recently gone through a divorce, and I didn't know if he was emotionally ready to embark on an international adventure with someone new.

"Wow, that sounds really fun," he said, followed by a pause that felt like an eternity. "Um, yeah, I think I can swing that. I'd love to go. Let's do it!"

"Really? Okay, great!" I said with a sigh of relief. "Let's talk about specifics tomorrow."

When I hung up the phone, a huge smile came across my face. I danced around my room and exclaimed, "Yes!"

The One-Two Punch

The next day, I woke up in a flurry of excitement about my adventure to Spain. I started searching the internet for flights, and I told my landlord that I'd be moving out on May 1, which was two months away.

I also took advantage of the remaining two months of my health insurance. I got on the phone and booked appointments with several of my doctors, even though I didn't have any symptoms.

On April 9, I saw my gynecologist.

"You're early," my doctor said while walking into the exam room. "You're not scheduled for your annual for another couple of months. Why are you here?"

"Well, I'm going on a big trip," I said, "so I thought I'd see my doctors before I go."

"Where are you going?" she said, as she began the routine breast exam.

"I'm going to Spain," I said, bubbling with excitement.

Suddenly, the doctor paused and began to press my right breast targeting one specific area near the armpit.

"What is it?" I asked.

"I feel something suspicious here," she said. "Have you had a mammogram lately?"

"No, I've never had one," I said. "Since cancer doesn't run in my family, my insurance doesn't cover mammograms until the age of forty-five. And, I'm forty-four now."

"Well, eighty percent of women who have breast cancer have no family history," she said. "It's time for that mammogram."

My eyes widened and my entire body froze on the medical bench. *It's time? She feels something suspicious? What is she talking about?*

After the doctor left, I got up from the bench, put on my clothes, and walked to the front desk to make an appointment for my first mammogram.

On the drive home, I was a ball of nerves. *What if there is something wrong? What if I have cancer? No, no that's impossible.*

I went straight into denial. It didn't make rational sense that I would be sick. I practiced yoga and meditation every day. I'd been a high-school biology teacher and a health journalist. I'd written countless articles about how to *prevent* cancer. Illness is what happened to other people—it would never happen to me.

The next day I returned to the radiation clinic for a 3-D mammogram and received my results a couple of days later. Sure enough, the mammogram revealed two masses in my right breast. Immediately after getting the results, I called my Mom in a panic.

"Mom, the mammogram shows two lumps," I said, completely freaking out. "What do you think they are? Do you think it could be cancer?"

"Oh, don't worry, honey, fibroids run in the family. It's all the coffee you drink," said Mom. "Just think about your trip. In a few short weeks, you'll be in Spain, having the time of your life."

"Okay, okay. Yeah, I'm sure that's all it is," I said, with a forced laugh. "Alright, well, I'll call you later. I have so much to do right now, both for my trip and for moving."

As a way to maintain a sense of control over my uncertain health, I kept an attitude of denial. Along with booking movers and buying supplies for trekking the Camino, scheduling doctor's appointments was just another part of my to-do list.

On April 24, I returned to the clinic for a biopsy. I chatted with the doctor about my upcoming trip to Spain and that I was planning to buy my plane ticket that afternoon. The doctor gave me a brief smile, then continued focusing on her work.

As I laid on my back on the medical bench, I shifted my attention to the ultrasound screen. I saw two hot-dog shaped masses with a link between them forming a barbell shape. My ob-gyn said this particular shape was indicative of HER2 breast cancer, a rare type that grows quickly.

That vision on the ultrasound screen shook me to the core. Suddenly, malignancy was in the realm of possibility.

I looked up at my doctor, and asked, "Should I not buy my plane ticket today?" There was a long pause.

"You're going to need more tests," she said, with sadness in her eyes. She already knew.

Any pause in the planning of my move or my trip was an acknowledgment that I might have cancer. And since that was certainly not happening (there was no possible way I had cancer!), I continued down my to-do list as if everything was fine.

April 30 was packing day, and movers were arriving the next morning. As Mom and I were sorting and packing my belongings into cardboard boxes strewn all over the house, the phone rang. I searched for my phone and spotted it on the kitchen table.

I saw on my phone's screen that it was my doctor. I took a deep breath and answered the phone.

"Hello, Sharon?" asked my doctor.

"Yes, this is Sharon," I replied.

"I have your biopsy results," she said.

"Okay," I said, and took a seat.

Then, I heard the words that are everyone's worst nightmare.

"I'm so sorry, Sharon. You have cancer," she said.

I went into shock. As if having a bird's-eye-view, I was looking down at myself on the phone. The experience was surreal as if something out of a movie. Everything was happening in slow motion.

Holding the phone to my ear, my consciousness returned to my body, and I looked at the cardboard boxes surrounding me. *This is not happening. I am moving out tomorrow and going on a romantic trip to Spain in a couple weeks. I don't have time for cancer!*

A tidal wave of dread and panic replaced the noise in my head. I couldn't catch my breath, my heart began to race, and I suddenly became nauseous.

The doctor continued, "You have an appointment tomorrow with your UCLA team of physicians. They will provide you with next steps. Will you be there? Sharon, are you there? Are you okay?"

"Yes, I'm here," I stuttered. "Yes, I'll be at those appointments tomorrow."

I hung up the phone. My body was frozen to the chair.

Mom came into the kitchen carrying a pile of my clothes. "Where should I put these, honey?" she asked.

With a glazed look on my face, I turned to her and said, "Mom, I have cancer."

Chapter 2
All the Doctors

"It is important to expect nothing, to take every experience, including the negative ones, as merely steps on the path. Suffering is part of our training program for becoming wise."
Ram Dass, spiritual teacher

How to make God laugh? Make plans

After that phone call, everything changed. That call marked the moment I realized that I don't have control over what happens in my life. I was humbled to the core. I put down my to-do list—a tangible representation of the illusion of control—and felt a whirlwind of sensations in my body.

"How about we go for a walk?" Mom said, holding out her hand. "Let's get some fresh air."

I nodded and took her hand. We walked to the beach and sat down on the warm sand. It was a beautiful evening and the sun was about to set on the ocean.

My state of shock shifted into anger.

"How did this happen?" I asked Mom. "I've done everything right. I exercise, I meditate, I get the salad on the side when I really want French fries. And for what? Just to *die*? I'm getting the fries from now on!"

"Yes, of course," Mom said. I looked into her eyes and asked, "Mom, why did this happen?"

Mom could not find the words to comfort me, so instead, she held out her arms, and I fell into her embrace. As we sat there looking at the gorgeous sunset, vibrant with salmon-colored clouds and iridescent reflections on the water, the fear of death spiraled within me like a tornado.

After ten minutes of crying, I paused. I suddenly had a new perspective—the fragility of life came into focus.

Growing up, I'd always been an overachiever—getting straight As, being the student-body president and captain of the volleyball team. For my entire life, I'd put so much pressure on myself to get things "just right." But in that moment, I realized my life could be over in an instant, so why was I so hard on myself? *What was I trying to prove?*

It all seemed so trivial now. I could die today, and all of that effort to win people over would be for nothing; I would have lived a life in pursuit of others' approval rather than living a life true to myself.

My mind was a whirlwind of fear and confusion, but there was one thing that was crystal clear—*I do not have control in this life.*

My phone buzzed. It was a text from Will.

"Hey, Sharon, did you get the results yet?" the text read. I couldn't respond at that moment. Since the relationship was so new, I didn't know what his response would be, and I wasn't ready to field rejection in case he wanted to walk away.

I also had to accept that my dream of going to Spain was not happening. I wasn't going anywhere for a while. Life had a different plan for me. I would be taking an international trip, but going inward.

Mom and I walked to a little Italian restaurant around the corner and we indulged in pasta and wine. Lots of wine. And dessert. I never ordered dessert. But that night, I got the tiramisu, and it was fucking delicious.

Is This a Bad Dream?

The next morning, I woke up and thought, *Was it all a bad dream?* I sat up in bed and looked around. *No, this is actually happening.* My entire body tensed up in fear and resistance.

I walked into the living room and broke the news to my two housemates, Jared and Shalini. I asked if I could stay there while I went through treatment. They hadn't found a new housemate for my room, so it was okay for me to stay. They were incredibly kind and said they would support me through this challenging time. I promised that I would maintain a positive attitude and not bring negative energy into the home.

The three of us shared a hug and I felt a sense of relief. Any predictable element in my life provided a much-needed sense of safety. I was grateful for my home, with loving housemates, because it was something stable under my feet during such an uncertain time.

After two cups of coffee, I canceled the movers and the storage facility. I walked into my bedroom and closed the door. It was time to return Will's text from the night before.

"Hey, Will, sorry for the delay," I texted. "Unfortunately, we have to cancel the trip to Spain. The results were positive. I know we hardly know each other, and I know you didn't sign up for this, so if you want to walk away or just be friends, I completely understand."

Two seconds later, my phone rang.

"Hey," I answered, bracing myself for a breakup.

"Hey, Sharon," Will said, sweetly. "I'm so sorry. How are you holding up?"

"Oh, I don't know. I'm pretty rattled," I said.

"About your text, don't worry about that," he said. "I care about you. I want to keep seeing you. Don't worry, I'm here."

"Oh, thank you, Will," I said with tears welling up. I felt a wave of relief and an incredible appreciation for this man. "Thank you so much."

"Yeah, you've got this," he said. "You are one of the sweetest, most positive persons I have ever met. I can hardly imagine what strength and wisdom you'll have after this, given where you're starting from."

I took a deep breath, soaking in the kindness of his words.

"Thank you, love," I said, smiling. "Don't they say I'll transform into a butterfly or something?"

"Well, you're already a beautiful caterpillar," he replied. I swooned and wanted to stay in our bubble of sweetness forever.

"Sharon, we have to get going," called Mom from the living room.

"I've got to go," I said to Will. "I'm meeting all of my doctors today at UCLA."

"Okay, call me later?" he asked. "And don't worry, you're going to be okay."

As I heard those words, I appreciated the sentiment, but I wasn't so sure. At that point, I didn't know much about my cancer, but I was about to find out.

Mom and I drove to UCLA Medical Center to meet all of the doctors who would be on this journey with me. I walked down the hallway, scanning the signs on the doors. I stopped at the door marked "UCLA Oncology," and took a deep breath. I was officially an oncology patient—an identity I couldn't wrap my head around and fiercely resisted. As if in a horror movie, walking through that door was surreal, confusing, and sinister.

"Hi, Sharon. I'm Dr. Kelly McCann. Come on in," said my cheerful oncologist, who was wearing a cocktail dress and three-inch heels. Her big smile and positivity brought some sunshine to the dark cloud of my mind. She handed me an eight-page packet covering the results of my biopsy, my chemotherapy plan, and how to manage all of the side effects.

Mom and I sat down in Dr. McCann's office, and she explained the information in the packet, page by page. I couldn't focus on the conversation, and I was lost in my thoughts. *Is this actually happening? Is this for real?* Then, we got to page three, and there it was—the diagnosis in black and white:

Invasive ductal carcinoma of the right breast, ER- PR- HER2+

I dropped my face into my hands and began to cry. Dr. McCann paused and gave me a look of compassion. I took a deep breath, quietly sat up, and tried to center myself.

My doctor went on to discuss the pharmaceuticals involved in the treatment and how to manage the side effects. "Sharon, you have the most aggressive type of breast cancer, so we need to be aggressive with the treatment," my doctor said. "We're bringing in the big guns for your chemo."

I looked at the long list of drugs I'd be taking, then shook my head in anguish. Mom chimed in. "You're talking to someone who doesn't take aspirin for a headache."

With the exuberance of a cheerleader, Dr. McCann said, "No, you're good. You're going to be okay. Chemicals are amazing!"

Although I appreciated her positivity, I was in shock, in a state of confusion, and too overwhelmed to be reassured.

Dr. McCann explained that HER2 stood for human epidermal growth factor receptor two. She would need to conduct more tests to assess the stage and whether or not the cancer cells had metastasized. She also said that HER2 had an antidote, a medicine called Herceptin, which would be part of my five-month chemotherapy treatment.

"Can we finish reading the packet later?" I asked, feeling a bit nauseous.

"Of course," the doctor said with an understanding smile.

Mom and I walked out of the oncology building and paused briefly on the sidewalk. We made eye contact, but neither of us said a word. We both knew how much the other one was hurting. Mom grabbed my hand and we entered the building next door. We rode the elevator to the third floor to meet my breast surgeon.

In the waiting room, I saw a patient who had lost her hair. I touched my long, blonde hair, and thought, *That's going to be me.*

The nurse called me into the exam room.

My surgeon, Dr. Amy Kusske, entered the room with the swagger of a mama bear protecting her cubs. She had finished surgery that morning and was ready to focus on her next patient without skipping a beat. I marveled at her calm and powerful demeanor.

"You got laid off and then got diagnosed with cancer?" she asked, looking at my chart. "This has been a rough year for you."

"Yeah," I said, staring at the floor.

We discussed the surgical options of having a lumpectomy versus a mastectomy, as well as the necessity of removing lymph nodes. Again, it was challenging for me to focus on the conversation. We were discussing the possibility of losing parts of my body. And not just any parts—*lady parts*. I felt like I'd been punched in the stomach, and I could hardly breathe.

As we were wrapping up, I said, "There is a meditation retreat I'd like to go to next week. Should I go? Or should I start treatment right away?"

"Definitely go," she said. "The timing is fortuitous. This treatment journey is a marathon, and meditation can help."

On her way out, she stopped and looked me straight in the eyes. With the conviction of a commander in chief, she said, "Let's get you well."

I looked at Mom and whispered, "She's a badass."

The day was not over yet. Next, we met the plastic surgeon, Dr. Jason Roostaeian. He was an attractive man wearing thick, black-framed glasses, reminiscent of Clark Kent. I thought to myself, *Is my doctor Superman?*

With my plastic surgeon, Dr. Jason Roostaeian, M.D. UCLA Health.

"Hi, Sharon. It's nice to meet you," he said, extending a hand. His smile was so radiant, I forgot I had cancer for a moment.

"Thanks. You, too," I replied and shook his hand.

"I understand you're debating between having a mastectomy versus a lumpectomy," he said as he took a seat. "I think mastectomy would be the better option. Your tumors take up the space of about a fourth of your breast, so you may not be happy with how a lumpectomy would look. Reconstruction of the entire breast would look better."

The thought of my right breast being removed was devastating and beyond my comprehension. But I recalled a friend who also had HER2 breast cancer and opted for a lumpectomy, even when her doctor recommended a mastectomy. Her cancer returned a couple of years later and took her life.

"I'll have the mastectomy," I said, quickly. As horrendous as losing a breast sounded, losing my life was certainly worse.

How the plastic surgeon would reconstruct my new breast was the next decision to make. Most women in my position received a breast implant, however, Dr. Roostaeian offered an alternative. He specialized in a surgery called the DIEP flap, a procedure in which abdominal fat, as well as blood vessels called deep inferior epigastric perforators or DIEP, were transferred from the belly to the chest to reconstruct a new breast.

"So, with the DIEP flap procedure, my new breast would consist of my *own* fat tissue rather than an implant," I asked, "*and* I'd get a flat stomach?"

"Yes, that's right," he said with a smile. "But first, we have to make sure you have enough stomach fat to qualify for the procedure."

The doctor left the room, and I changed into a gown. I looked down at my belly pooch and for the first time in my life, I was happy with what I saw.

Dr. Roostaeian came back into the room and took a close look at my breasts and abdomen. Since he was so good looking, I turned bright red with embarrassment. Usually when an attractive man is looking at my breasts, we are in a dark and cozy bedroom, not a sterile, fluorescently-lit hospital room—*and my mother is certainly not in the room with us!*

The plastic surgeon cupped my stomach fat with his hand and said, "Yeah, there's enough fat there. That should work." My eyes widened when I realized that he was cupping my future breast. I looked at my mom, who seemed to read my mind and was about to burst into laughter.

The doctor took a step back and I closed my gown. He continued, "But you'll have to gain about ten pounds before surgery to have enough belly fat to create a C cup to match your other breast."

Wait, I have to gain *weight?* The thought of purposefully gaining weight was kind of … exciting. I began thinking about tiramisu, and my mouth started to water. Then, my mind quickly returned to the gravity of the situation.

"So, how often do you do this type of surgery?" I asked him. I didn't want to be one of his first cases for this innovative procedure.

"About once a week," he said, "for about five years now."

Okay, that's a relief. He was, after all, an accomplished plastic surgeon in Los Angeles, the land of perfect, surgically-enhanced breasts. I was in good hands with this doctor, but I'm sure my face still reflected my inner landscape of fear.

"Don't worry," he said on his way out of the exam room. "I'll make you beautiful."

The "What if...?" Nature of the Mind

Everything was happening so fast. In only a few hours, the doctors had scheduled every month of my life for an entire year. I would undergo five months of aggressive chemotherapy treatments, followed by a mastectomy of the right breast and removal of nine lymph nodes; then one month of radiation, and then six more months of chemotherapy. The final chemo treatment would be May 1, 2019, exactly one year away. Although it was only one year, given all of the unknowns on this path, it seemed like an eternity.

As I left the building, my mind was bouncing from one emotion to the next. I was still feeling disbelief about the diagnosis, anxiety about the treatments, but also gratitude for having access to such talented doctors. I was also calculating how much tiramisu I could eat to gain ten pounds in five months.

By the time I arrived home from the medical center, my mind had started to reel out of control. *What if the chemo doesn't work? What if the surgeries have complications? What if I don't survive this?*

As a meditation teacher, I knew that the mind defaults to worst-case scenarios for survival, so this string of "what if's ...?" was a natural program of the mind. The best thing I could do to settle my mind was to take a seat on my meditation cushion, close my eyes, and take a few deep breaths.

I had learned several different types of meditation over the years, and it was time to put them to the test. First, I tried sound meditation and listened to a CD of a repeating gong. I tried to concentrate on the sound, but my mind was still scattered in fear. I picked up my mala beads and chanted a mantra from my yoga training, but the chant didn't calm me down.

Then I recalled mindfulness, a practice from the Buddhist tradition in which the focus is on present-moment experiences, such as thoughts, emotions, and body sensations. A key premise of mindfulness is to accept our life circumstances just as they are.

Obviously, I wanted to change my circumstance, so I didn't think mindfulness would be that helpful. But feeling desperate and willing to try anything, I experimented with the mindfulness practice of "labeling" my thoughts and emotions.

And, then, something shifted.

Sitting on my meditation pillow, I took several deep breaths and witnessed my thoughts and emotions emerge. As if placing a Post-it note onto the emotion, I labeled it, "fear." Then I shifted my attention to the sensation of my breath going in and out of my nose.

I didn't judge the fact that I was experiencing fear. I didn't try to push the emotion away. Instead, I simply acknowledged its presence with this label, and then gently brought my focus back to the breath.

After about fifteen minutes, the emotion began to settle. The practice created a bit of space between me and the fear, and I experienced some perspective—I was no longer *in* the emotion; instead, I was observing it.

For the first time since my diagnosis, I felt a few seconds of peace.

I heard the chime of my twenty-minute timer. I opened my eyes, and thought, *This practice works! Even with cancer, my worst nightmare.*

I jumped up and ran into the living room with the excitement of a seven-year-old on Christmas morning. "Mom, I found the practice that works!" I said. "Mindfulness. It works!"

Chapter 3
The Label Practice—Label the Emotion

"I've had a lot of worries in my life, most of which never happened."
Mark Twain, author

The Wandering Mind

Anyone who has ever meditated has probably noticed the mind's tendency to wander. Our minds often re-run contentious conversations from the past, such as rehashing a discussion with our boss saying the things we *wish* we could say. Or, our thoughts travel to the future, making grocery lists, travel plans, or worrying about our finances. Whether we are ruminating on the past or rehearsing for the future, our minds are often in flux.

Our minds become present, however, when we are fully engaged in a conversation or concentrating on a particular task. But, when we are not doing something that requires our full attention, our minds are typically off to the races.

In a 2010 study, researchers found that participants' minds were wandering 46.9 percent of the time.[1] This study implies that we are not present for nearly *half* of our lives! Fortunately, mindfulness practice helps us be more present, not just during meditation but also when we are "off the cushion." Since it requires effort to corral the mind from the past or the future, the repeated effort we exert during mindfulness practice rewires the brain and increases our capacity to be more present in our daily lives.[2]

It's important not to judge ourselves when our minds drift during meditation. There is an evolutionary reason for the wandering nature of the mind—the human brain is hardwired to be on alert for threats constantly. Just like the heart's job is to circulate blood to keep us alive, the mind's role is to think, defend itself, and anticipate danger.

Mind-wandering is especially noticeable during meditation since we're not focused on a specific task. Therefore, it's important to remember that it's natural for our minds to wander while we are sitting in meditation so that we don't think we are doing the meditation wrong or that we are "bad" meditators.

The Neuroscience of the Wandering Mind

When our minds wander, the part of the brain that is activated is called the default mode network (DMN), a network of interacting regions located down the midline of the brain. Since it takes effort to be present, but it is effort*less* for our thoughts to drift into the past or future, the wandering mind is our "default" mental state.[3]

The DMN creates a sense of self, projects this self into the past or future, and searches for problems to fix, manage, or control. This part of the brain creates "movies" in the mind, rehashing anger-filled conversations from the past or projecting anxiety-ridden scenes in the future.

The DMN continually surveys our experiential landscape for potential threats. It conjures up worst-case scenarios so that our minds can predict—and hopefully avoid—threatening situations.

For example, let's say an attractive person starts working with your spouse. As your beloved leaves for work, your DMN may create a mind-movie starring your partner flirting with this new employee, leaving you pacing around the house filled with anxiety and jealousy. Perhaps one-in-ten times, your spouse is indeed flirting with the co-worker (a-ha! The story is correct!), however, the vast majority of the time, this isn't the case, and we suffer for no good reason.

The DMN is not all bad—it's what kept our ancestors alive. Early humans lived in a treacherous environment, and those who consistently predicted danger were more likely to survive. Hence, those with a stronger DMN passed their genes onto the next generation.

Even though our current environment does not pose as many life-threatening possibilities as early humans encountered, our brain's survival mechanisms were established during that time. We are using stone-age brains in a modern environment, which is causing an immense amount of needless suffering.

Having an overactive DMN is also known as being hypervigilant, or constantly "on guard." Mindfulness can help us bring awareness to these anger- or anxiety-provoking thoughts created by the DMN. This allows us to gain perspective, recognize when we've projected our fears or created a false story, and alleviate unnecessary stress in our lives.[4] In a moment of anxiety about the future, we can ask ourselves, "Is this outcome realistic, or is this fear a result of my DMN projecting or overreacting?"

Anchoring Our Minds into the Present Moment

It's been said that meditation is simple, but not easy. The concept of meditation may be straightforward (aren't we just sitting on a cushion being present?), but since the natural tendency of our minds is to wander, maintaining presence requires a considerable amount of effort.

Luckily, we can use a meditation anchor to help stabilize our minds. A meditation anchor functions in a similar way as a ship anchor. When a boat is tossed and turned by ocean waves, the captain can drop an anchor to steady the ship in one place.

In mindfulness practice, we use a meditation anchor to drop and fasten our minds into the present moment. With the use of a meditation anchor, we can maintain a calm state of presence, even among the most tumultuous of environments.

There are many different types of meditation anchors from various spiritual traditions. For example, in yogic practices, there are several sacred images as well as mantras (repeated words or phrases) to help anchor the mind into the present moment.

Anchors typically used in mindfulness meditation are the breath, body sensations, and listening to sounds. Focusing on one of these three anchors brings the mind into the present because they are inseparable from the body—and the body always resides in the present moment.

The breath is the most common of the three because most people feel neutral about their breath. But it's good to know that focusing on sound or body sensations are great alternatives if focusing on the breath doesn't feel good for any reason. The key is to do what feels comfortable so that our nervous systems can fully relax.

Respond vs. React

Researchers found that when participants were in the present moment, that is, focused on a task or doing a mindfulness exercise, their DMN became inactive, and their past-and-future thoughts disappeared.[5] Therefore, mindfulness gives our mind a break from the network's incessant thoughts, allowing us to experience the ease and peacefulness of the present moment.

Instead of being lost in the emotion, we recognize that we are *having* an emotion. This realization creates spaciousness in the mind, and provides perspective and clarity on a potential threat. Rather than spiraling in the hurricane, with mindfulness, we become the eye of the storm.

Mindfulness practice deactivates another part of the brain's survival mechanism: the amygdala. This almond-shaped structure registers danger and triggers the body's stress responses of fight, flight, or freeze. The amygdala is an ancient brain structure that evolved in animals previous to early humans.[6]

UCLA researchers found that when participants utilized the mindfulness practice of "labeling," brain activity shifted from the amygdala (located in the center of the brain) to the prefrontal cortex (located just behind the forehead).[7] The prefrontal cortex is the site of reasoning in the brain, therefore mindfulness helps us to calmly *respond* to a given challenge rather than *react* from our amygdala.

The Mindful Gap

When we shift from our amygdala to the prefrontal cortex, we experience a break in our stressful thinking, or a "mindful gap."

For example, let's say we receive a critical email from our boss and our amygdala is triggered. Without mindfulness, we may react and send an angry email in return, which could result in a negative consequence. But, if we bring mindfulness to our angry emotion, we can shift our brain activity from our amygdala to our prefrontal cortex, and experience the pause of the "mindful gap." Since we are now operating from our prefrontal cortex, we can respond to our boss from a more balanced and reasonable state of mind.

The Mindful Gap: **Mindfulness Provides Space between Stimulus and Response**
Without Mindfulness: Critical email from boss (stimulus) –> Amygdala triggers –> React from a place of upset (response) –> Negative consequence
With Mindfulness: Critical email from boss (stimulus) –> Amygdala triggers, but then is deactivated with mindfulness practice –> **The Mindful Gap** –> Prefrontal cortex is activated –> Respond from a place of reasoning (response) –> Positive consequence

Although the amygdala has helped humans survive over millennia, this brain structure does not discern whether or not a danger is life-threatening. Whether we receive a scathing email from our boss or a lion is chasing us on the African savanna, the amygdala flips like a light switch just the same.

Spending too much time in this hypervigilant—always "on guard"—mental state may cause the amygdala's "switch" to flip too quickly. For many people, being "easily triggered" has become a mental habit creating an enormous amount of unnecessary suffering.

When we bring mindfulness to a challenging situation, we can switch our amygdala to the "off" position, put down our defenses, and see the circumstance more clearly. With daily mindfulness practice, our self-awareness increases, and we begin to identify when we are operating from our primitive survival mechanisms versus our more evolved prefrontal cortex. We can catch ourselves when we start to behave according to old patterns, take a deep breath, and then make a different choice.

Knowing that our DMN is always running and our amygdala will always be ready to flip, we must put in a conscious effort to be present throughout the day. With greater awareness, we start to realize that most of life's challenges are not life-threatening, and we begin to calm these antiquated, survival-related brain structures. With mindfulness, we can cultivate a less-reactive mindset, and experience more peace and presence in our lives.

Name It to Tame It

The Label practice, also known as "noting" or "naming," is an exercise that uses the wandering nature of the mind to strengthen our ability to be mindful. Every time the mind wanders, we are presented with an opportunity to create a label, and the stronger our mindfulness becomes.

The Label meditation begins by focusing our minds on the sensation of the breath moving in and out of the nostrils. Whenever a thought appears in the mind, we can simply label it "thought" and then return our focus back to the breath.

Even though emotions have more charge than thoughts, the Label practice works in the same way. When an emotion arises during meditation, we can meet the emotion with full attention, give it a label such as "fear," then bring the mind back to the breath. When we label our emotions, we are also increasing our emotional intelligence since we are honing the skill of accurately identifying emotions within ourselves and others.

One definition of mindfulness is paying attention to our experience *as it's happening*. When we feel angry, we can label our experience "anger is present." The Label practice allows us to acknowledge that anger is in our experience in the actual moment the emotion is occurring.

It's important not to identify with the emotion by saying, "I feel angry." Instead, we can use labels such as "anger is here" or "anger is rising," which distinguish the feeling as a separate entity. The act of labeling creates a sense of space between ourselves and the emotion. It may be helpful for us to imagine using a mental Post-it note to visualize the thought or emotion as something separate from ourselves.

Sometimes it's difficult to put a word to what we are feeling. So, below is a chart of possible labels to help us identify our emotions. When practicing the Label meditation, it is better to choose a label that is more specific than general. For example, "frustration" would be a better label than "anger." Also, it is common to experience more than one emotion at any given time, but for the sake of this exercise, choose only one emotion to work with.

Emotion Category	Possible Labels
Anger	frustration, irritation, resentment, annoyance, disappointment, rage, betrayal, disrespect, agitation, impatience, crankiness
Fear	anxiety, confusion, lost, craving, panic, terror, worry, discomfort
Sadness	depression, discouragement, grief, disillusionment, loneliness, hurt
Disgust	embarrassment, shame, judgment, guilt, hate, aversion, jealousy, suspicion

Lastly, it's important not to judge the emotion that arises. Anger is an emotion that we often judge ourselves for having, but the emotion itself is neutral—it's what we do with it that can be problematic.

Before we start, let's draw a parallel between the Label practice and weight lifting. Every time the mind wanders and we create a label and direct the mind back to the breath, it's as if we have performed a "rep"—we are building the "muscle" of mindfulness. Also, similar to lifting weights, the Label exercise gets easier with consistent practice. But instead of building muscles in our physical bodies, we are building concentration, self-awareness, and a nonreactive mind.

The Label Practice Meditation

Listen to the meditation online at:
www.meditationforbreastcancer.com

Begin by gently closing your eyes or lowering your gaze to the floor. Bring both feet flat on the ground. Take a moment to lift your spine upright and relax your shoulders, arms and back. Relaxing the muscles of your face. Allowing your hands to rest wherever they are comfortable. Take a few deep breaths, allowing your body to soften.

Let your breath be natural, breathing in and out through the nose. Bringing your attention to your abdomen, notice your breath. Don't try to lengthen the breath, just notice the natural breath. Notice how your abdomen expands on the inhale and contracts on the exhale.

Now bring your attention to your chest and notice your breath in the chest area. Feel your chest rising and falling with each breath. On the inhale, the chest rises, on the exhale the chest falls. Continue to notice the breath at your chest area.

Now bring your attention to your breath flowing in and out of the nose. Focusing your concentration, feel the sensation of air coming in and out of the nostrils. Experience the temperature of the breath, perhaps it is cooler when you inhale, and warmer when you exhale. Focusing your attention on the breath flowing in and out of the nose.

Between the abdomen, the chest, and the nostrils, choose one of these three areas to focus on the breath. One is not better than the other, so don't worry about making the wrong choice. Just choose one. Now see if you can sustain your attention on the breath flowing in and out of that area. This area is your meditation anchor because it anchors your mind into the present moment. Continuing to breathe, focusing on your anchor, establishing your anchor for this meditation session.

When your mind starts to wander from the breath, you may start thinking about conversations from your past or things that may happen in the future. When you notice you're having a thought, simply give it the label "thinking," and then return your focus back to your breath, back to your anchor.

Emotions may also arise. When you notice that you're experiencing an emotion, also give it a label, such as "anger is rising," or "sadness is here," then gently bring your attention back to the breath. It's important not to identify with the emotions, so rather than say, "I am angry" use the label "anger is here." These labels create some space between you and your thoughts and emotions, and helps you to experience them as something separate from yourself.

I invite you to continue the Label practice on our own for the next five minutes. Remember that it takes effort and concentration to bring the wandering mind back to the breath, and your mind might get tired. But I'd like you to consider this practice to be similar to lifting weights in a gym. It takes effort and concentration to build muscles in the body. Similarly, when we are doing the Label practice, we are building the muscle of mindfulness.

Now set an intention to focus for a solid five minutes doing the Label practice. Start by focusing on your breath at your anchor. You may begin.

Remember, that when the mind wanders, you're not doing anything wrong–it's completely natural. Every time your mind wanders, you give it a label and then bring your attention back to the breath, you have completed a "rep" and you are growing the muscle of mindfulness.

Continue with the practice.

No matter how many times the mind wanders, there is nothing wrong, the mind is just doing its job. Just like the heart's job is to beat and circulate blood, the mind's job is to wander into the past and future to predict threat and keep us safe. This is why this practice takes so much effort. But the more times the mind wanders, the more "reps" you get to do, and your ability to be present becomes stronger. Continue with the practice.

In these last couple of minutes, I invite you to keep your eyes closed but let go of the Label practice. Just let your mind go wherever it wants to go. And now, notice, where does it go? Is there a certain conversation your mind is rehashing? Or a certain event your mind is worrying about that might happen in the future? There is nothing right or wrong, just notice where the mind naturally goes when it's not present.

Taking in a deep breath, feeling the sensation in the abdomen and chest expanding as you breathe in and contracting as you breath out. Taking two more deep breaths, inhaling through the nose, and exhaling out the mouth, releasing all of that effort. As we bring our meditation to a close, notice how you're feeling. How is your body feeling? How is your mind? Notice your feet on the floor. Feel your legs on the chair or cushion. Feel your hands on your lap. Whenever you're ready, take one last breath, and gently open your eyes.

Part 2
"O" *is for* Observe

Chapter 4

The Difference between Pain and Suffering

"God, grant me the serenity to accept the things I cannot change, the courage to change the things I can, and the wisdom to know the difference."
Reinhold Niebuhr, theologian

Big Sur

Despite being a trained meditation practitioner, before my cancer diagnosis, I was a bad-weather meditator. I meditated when I didn't feel good—when I was cranky, anxious, or depressed. I practiced meditation because I was interested in learning about spirituality and about the mind, but not necessarily to reduce suffering.

Meditating during my journey with cancer, however, was completely different. I couldn't *not* meditate. I was experiencing a higher level of anxiety than I had ever experienced before, and the only respite I had from this intense fear was during my mindfulness practice.

I meditated in twenty-minute sessions multiple times throughout the day. If a few hours went by when I didn't meditate, the "what if…?" part of my mind would escalate to overwhelming proportions—my fear of death would overtake me, and I wouldn't be able to get out of bed.

Five days after my diagnosis, I flew to Big Sur to attend a week-long meditation retreat that focused on mindfulness and self-compassion. Coincidently, I had signed up for this course about six months prior, and this incredible tool could not have come into my life at a better time.

The coastal retreat center was a beautiful place to connect to nature and hopefully gain some clarity around how I would approach this harrowing situation. I told the three teachers of the course what I was going through so they would understand if I left the room crying at any moment, which, indeed, was a regular occurrence throughout the week.

During a one-on-one session with one of the teachers, I had a breakthrough that changed everything.

"This diagnosis is activating your fear of death, but it most likely won't be the *cause* of your death," my teacher said. "Even though you have a cancer diagnosis, I might die before you. I may get hit by a bus tomorrow. Everyone will die someday and nobody knows when it will happen."

With this teaching, I learned to separate my diagnosis from my fear of death and to see them as two distinct concepts.

Being only forty-four years old and having been healthy all of my life, it was the first time I had experienced the fear of death. I had felt other strong emotions, such as heartache after a breakup or grief after the loss of a loved one, but the intensity of this fear was much greater than any other emotion I'd had in the past.

With past hardships, I had turned to meditation to reduce my suffering. It was time to trust these tools once again. As a trained meditation teacher, I knew what to do. It was just a matter of doing it, trusting the process, and being open to what my daily practice would reveal.

Pain Is Inevitable; Suffering Is Optional

During my retreat, I learned the difference between pain and suffering, a foundational teaching in Buddhist philosophy. Pain was something I didn't have control over, such as someone cutting me off on the freeway, getting laid off from work, or the fact that there were cancer cells in my body.

Suffering, on the other hand, was created by my *reaction* to the pain. I realized that it was not cancer itself that was causing my suffering, it was my *reaction* to having cancer that caused my suffering.

Although I didn't have control over my diagnosis, I did have control over my reaction. The meditation techniques I was learning at the retreat helped me cultivate a less-reactive relationship with having cancer.

My teacher shared the Buddhist parable "The Second Arrow." The parable illustrated the idea of being struck by two arrows, one at a time—the first arrow being the pain and the second arrow being the suffering (or the reaction to the pain). The teacher read the parable to the class:

"The Buddha once asked a student, 'If a person is struck by an arrow, is it painful?' The student replied, 'It is.' The Buddha then asked, 'If the person is struck by a second arrow, is that even more painful?' The student replied again, 'It is.' The Buddha then explained, 'In life, we cannot always control the first arrow. However, the second arrow is our reaction to the first. And with this second arrow comes the possibility of choice.'"

My teacher concluded that adversity was something everyone faced in their lives. Our character was not defined by what happens to us; rather it was determined by how we react to difficult times.

Sitting in class, I started to feel frustrated. *How do I not throw the second arrow? I don't need parables; I need practical tools to reduce this crippling fear that feels like an earthquake in my body!*

Holding back tears, I left the meditation hall and walked outside to an expansive lawn overlooking the ocean. Tension seized the muscles in my neck and stomach. I collapsed on the grassy lawn and began to cry. The mountains behind me were so massive that I felt like a small child cradled in the loving arms of mother earth.

Looking up at the mountains, I whispered, "God, am I going to die?" I closed my eyes and listened. I felt a cool breeze on my cheeks, and this message came to my heart:

You're going to be okay. You are held and supported. Connect to the Spirit within you. Use your tools.

I inhaled that heavenly message of reassurance with a deep breath and laid down on the cool grass. Soaking in warm rays from the sun and grounding support from the earth, I repeated to myself, *I'm going to be okay. I am held and supported. I'm going to be okay. I am held and supported.*

That afternoon, I thought more about the "The Second Arrow" parable, and I came up with a plan about how I was going to approach cancer treatment. As if creating two "buckets" in my mind, I separated the pain (the cancer cells in my body) from the suffering (my reaction to those cells). I gave the responsibility of the pain "bucket" to my doctors—they were in charge of getting the cancer out of my body. But the suffering "bucket" was *my* responsibility. Whether or not I suffered was *my* job. I had the meditation tools. I knew what to do. It was just about doing it.

I searched for a shady spot in which to meditate. I returned to the verdant, expansive lawn and sat down beneath a Monterey Cypress tree. In my earlier session, my mindfulness teacher said to me, "Observe as much as you can. Whatever comes up, just observe it."

These words were so simple, yet so profound. It was time to take my teacher's advice and commit to a daily practice.

Okay, this is real, and I'm doing it, I thought to myself, lifting my chest with strength. *I am committed to going through this journey with as much grace, courage, and self-love as possible.*

With a fierce level of determination, I crossed my legs, sat up tall in a noble meditation posture, and observed the hurricane of anxiety raging in my psyche.

With Mom in Big Sur.

Chapter 5
Living with Uncertainty

*"What I know, is that I don't know. Now I dance
and I sing and I live full. I give it all to the call of the
unknown. What I say, is that I don't say. Now I rest,
no stress, in the Holy Name. All fears and my tears
give it all away, I play like a child of the earth."*
Trevor Hall, singer-songwriter

All the Tests

I had never really believed in fate, but how everything was unfolding felt like destiny. The only reason I went to my gynecologist (who discovered the tumors) was because I'd been laid off and I would soon lose my health insurance. *Thank God I was laid off!*

The day after I returned from the meditation retreat, I began a series of diagnostic tests at UCLA Medical Center to reveal the severity of my condition, including the stage. I was hoping for the best, preparing for the worst, and trying to build inner strength with my meditation practice.

My mind was constantly flooded with fearful thoughts. *What are these tests going to reveal? Has the cancer spread to my lymph nodes or the rest of my body? What if I'm stage two, or worse?*

Rather than engage with these thoughts, I did my best just to observe them come and go in my mind. It was during this time of being in limbo and not having all of the answers that I learned how to live with uncertainty. I continually repeated to myself, *Whatever the tests reveal, I will take the next best step. I am supported. I am held. I will be okay.*

On May 15, I went to the medical center for an ultrasound. As the doctor circled the cold gel and ultrasound wand on my right breast, I saw the two tumors on the gray-scale screen. My eyes began to tear up. But this time they weren't tears about cancer; they were tears of grief around motherhood.

Before my diagnosis, I had hoped that my next ultrasound would be looking at a growing baby in my uterus, not growing tumors in my breast. The vision of the ultrasound was not only visual proof that two malignant tumors were in my body, but it was also a stark reminder that I was not a mother, something I'd always wanted in my life.

I felt jealous of the other women in the ultrasound clinic who were there to look at their developing babies. I recalled many of my friends sharing photographs of their ultrasounds, referring to the growing fetus as their little "peanut." Here I was, age forty-four, looking at the ultrasound image of my two, little peanut-sized tumors.

My oncologist had told me that I would most likely lose my fertility with chemotherapy. "You're right on the cusp," she said. "Chemotherapy will stop your period, and given that you're forty-four now, it may or may not come back."

The realities of both having cancer and not being a mother hit hard. I also feared that Will might leave me if I wasn't able to give birth to his children. Immense fear of losing Will filled my body, and I began to cry silently on the exam table.

As I walked out of the medical center, I realized that I had to put my dream of motherhood aside and focus on my own health. So, I shifted my priority from giving birth to a new life to surviving my own. *How could I be a mother if I don't survive?*

From Bad to Worse

Going in for tests, then waiting for results. Going in for tests, then waiting for results—this was my life during the four weeks of May. To cope, I meditated every morning and thought to myself, *Whatever happens today, the sun came up, and I'm grateful for that. I am able to take a deep breath, and I'm thankful for that. I am alive, and I'm grateful for that.*

I practiced mindfulness as a formal exercise every morning as well as informally throughout the day. I observed myself walking into medical buildings, going into MRI machines, and getting blood drawn. I observed my thoughts and emotions as I received emails that contained test results. I made a conscious effort to smile and say "thank you" to every nurse and every doctor—a practice that helped me stay present and grateful.

On May 22, I received the news that broke my equanimous flow. I was driving to the Hollywood Bowl to see Paul Simon in concert. It was Mom's birthday, and this concert was my gift to her. Looking at my phone, I noticed that I had received an email from my doctor with the MRI and lymph-node biopsy results. These results would reveal the stage of my cancer. I said a little prayer, hoping that the cancer was at stage one since that meant I wouldn't need chemotherapy.

I pulled over and opened the email on my phone. The tests confirmed two malignant tumors in my right breast, 2.3 and 1.6 centimeters in length. In between the tumors was a precancerous mass of calcification, creating a barbell shape, typical of HER2 cell growth. The barbell spanned 6.1 centimeters. I quickly did the math. *Whoa, I have a mass that is two-and-a-half inches wide in my breast!*

The tests also showed that cancer cells were in one of my lymph nodes, which categorized my case as stage two since malignancy had grown beyond the boundary of the breast. I squinted my eyes, cringed my shoulders and screamed inside my car, "Fuck!"

I put my phone down, took a couple of deep breaths, and got back on the freeway. The man in the car behind me blared his horn and then zoomed around me, flashing his middle finger in my direction.

That's when I completely lost it. All of the emotions from a month of testing, and then receiving the disappointing results, came to a head. "Fuck you, you fucking asshole!" I screamed, flipping my middle finger right back at him. As his car sped up and out of sight, I looked down at my speedometer and saw that I was driving only forty miles an hour.

I shook my head, surprised and ashamed of my behavior. I'd never had road rage like that before. I didn't typically cuss, but ever since receiving the diagnosis I was swearing like a sailor. I quickly offered myself some compassion. *This is a really hard time. It's okay if I get angry. I'm a meditation teacher, but I'm also a human being.*

After an hour of LA traffic, I arrived at the concert and met my parents. I tried to keep my anxiety under control, but I felt like a shaken can of soda ready to burst. I didn't want to ruin Mom's birthday, so I kept the test results to myself. About midway through the concert, Paul Simon performed his song "The Sound of Silence," and when he sang the lyric "silence like a cancer grows," I couldn't hold back the tears. I realized the best thing I could do for me, and everyone around me, was to excuse myself and do my practice.

Tears were already flowing, so I grabbed a handful of napkins from the concession stand and found a secluded bench. Mom followed me, and I told her about my test results.

"I found out that I'm stage two," I said, sobbing. "I'm going to need chemo." Mom's jaw dropped and she said, "Oh no...."

"I can't talk about it right now," I said, interrupting her. "I just need to do my practice." Mom held back her words and we both sat down on the bench. I sat up tall, took a deep breath, and closed my eyes.

Napkins in hand, I whispered to myself, "Label. Anxiety is rising. Anxiety is here. Observe. Observe the anxiety. Where is it in my body? I feel anxiety in my neck. It's now in my abdomen—just observe it. The emotion is neither good nor bad—just observe it. I'm not pushing it away. The anxiety can stay as long as it needs to."

"You're going to be okay, honey," Mom said, trying to make me feel better.

"It's okay, Mom, crying is part of the practice," I said. "You don't need to try and make me feel better. The emotion is like a weather pattern. Watch, it will pass. Like a storm that wells up, the emotion will stay for a bit, but then it passes. Just hold space for me, okay?"

Mom nodded and then sat up tall and opened up her hands to energetically hold me with compassion. It was hard to watch her baby cry, but she trusted me and this meditative process.

Comparable to a tornado swirling across the countryside, anxiety arose in my body, was very intense and lingered for some time, and then swirled out of my experience.

After about ten minutes of practice, I opened my teary eyes, looked at Mom, and said, "Okay, I'm ready to enjoy the concert now."

She gave me a knowing smile. "I'm so proud of you," she said. "You've got this."

We walked arm-in-arm back to our seats. Since I'd done my practice and let go of my anxiety, I was able to enjoy the rest of the concert. Which was a good thing because Mom's favorite song, "Diamonds on the Soles of her Shoes," was up next, and we danced our little hearts out.

Letting Go of Having to Know "Why"

The next day, I was trying to figure out what had caused my diagnosis. At sunset, I took a solo walk to the beach to find some peace. On a biological level, I knew that stress created cortisol and inflammation in the body, which is linked to cancer. Sure, I had a stressful job, but I knew hundreds of other people who had much more stressful jobs than mine. The truth was, there was no clear reason.

By the time I hit the sand, my mind was spinning so fast that I fell to my knees in a state of despair. *Why did this happen? What did I do wrong? What did I do to deserve this? Was it because I drank too much wine? Was it because I never forgave my father? Was I exposed to a virus or chemical in my childhood?*

I listened for an answer, but I got nothing. I dropped my head into my hands and released a flood of tears.

When the tears stopped, I took a breath and looked up at the moon and the emerging stars in the sky. The intensity of my pain cracked open my heart, and I connected with the astounding beauty of the full moon.

I visualized the moon orbiting the earth, and then the earth orbiting the sun. Then I imagined the elegance of our solar system spiraling in our galaxy. I closed my eyes and connected to the divine forces that orchestrate the celestial perfection of the universe.

My mind dropped into a profound expansiveness within my chest—a place of deep stillness and peace. For a brief moment, I became aware of the vastness of it all. At that moment, I knew that I had done nothing wrong and that I was deeply loved.

Not being part of a specific religion, I wasn't sure how to define or what to call this divine consciousness that I had tapped into. All I knew was getting cancer had brought me to my knees, searching for guidance and answers. I had so many questions that my mortal mind would never have definitive answers for, but I believed that the omniscient Spirit knew why I got cancer. And for that reason, I bowed down to this divine mystery, right there on the beach underneath the starry sky, and prayed:

I don't know why I got cancer, but you do, and for that reason, I surrender to you. Help me to learn the lessons from this experience so that I may better serve others. I trust you. I trust this process. And, I surrender.

Then a wave of comfort washed over me, and I let go of the need to know "why." I knew that getting cancer happened for a reason—and this reason would reveal itself when the time was right. I realized that each challenge in life could inspire me to look inward and connect to my Spirit, as well as develop more compassion for myself and others.

Unexpectedly, in my state of full surrender, I didn't feel weak. On the contrary, I felt safe, strong, and at peace.

Chapter 6
The Observe Practice— Observe the Emotion

"To transform our suffering, we don't struggle with it or try to get rid of it. We simply bathe it in the light of our mindfulness."
Thich Nhat Hanh, spiritual teacher

The Two Minds

When we sit to meditate, we experience our wandering minds almost immediately. This mental chatter is known as the "thinking mind." The thinking mind includes all our thoughts and emotions, and is continually trying to fix, manage, and control our life's situations.

During meditation, we do our best to observe the thinking mind. And this begs the question, "Who is doing the observing?" It becomes clear that there is a second consciousness, or the "observing mind."

Similar to the Label practice, the Observe practice creates a "mindful gap" between ourselves and the emotion. This space allows us to no longer identify with the emotion, which lessens the charge and allows inner peace to emerge.

Observe Sensations in the Body

Another way to calm our minds with the Observe practice is to locate emotions in our bodies, which often take the form of bodily sensations. For example, rather than getting caught up in our angry thoughts, we can focus on the bodily sensations that are related to the anger, such as, *I feel heat in my face, tension in my shoulders, and a rapid heart rate.*

When we get out of our heads and into our bodies, our minds usually experience some peace. Most of us have had this peaceful experience while doing yoga or dancing to beautiful music—when we not only hear, but we also *feel* the music. In meditation practice, we can consciously direct our attention to our bodily sensations and experience the same feeling of ease.

In her book *Fully Present,* nationally-known mindfulness teacher Diana Winston says the technique of focusing on bodily sensations is particularly helpful when we have repetitive or obsessive thoughts. Winston says that repetitive thoughts are often fueled by challenging emotions that reside in our bodies. For example, underlying anxiety can fuel constant worries about the future, and unresolved anger can fuel ongoing resentments about the past.

Fortunately, mindfulness provides the tools to stop these repetitive loops of thinking. When challenging emotions arise, we can choose to focus on the accompanying bodily sensations rather than the circling of thoughts, which typically calms down the mind. Winston says, "By placing your attention on bodily sensations rather than on the story you are telling yourself, you can relax a bit, and thinking may even stop on its own."

Emotions Are like the Weather

When the observing mind watches the thinking mind, we may notice the temporal nature of our thoughts and emotions. Similar to weather patterns, thoughts and emotions spiral into our experience, stay for a bit, and eventually drift away on their own.

When we step back and observe, we are able to see emotions for what they actually are—*energies in motion.* When we are experiencing a bout of sadness, for example, it may seem like the gloominess will be there forever. But like a heavy rainstorm, the dark clouds of sorrow eventually subside.

We typically don't need to wait very long for this dark cloud to pass. In her book *My Stroke of Insight*, neuroscientist Jill Bolte-Taylor says the lifespan of an emotion is only 90 seconds. To put this in context, one angry thought can trigger a surge of adrenaline in the muscles, a rapid heart rate, and heat in the face—all of which escalate, come to a peak, and then dissipate within 90 seconds. If we have additional angry thoughts, this chain of physical sensation repeats.

Another way to think about this concept is to imagine our observing mind as the blue sky, and our thoughts and emotions are like clouds drifting across the atmosphere. The blue sky doesn't judge the clouds or try to make them move faster or slower. Instead, it serves as the backdrop for the clouds to express themselves and then dissipate in their own way and in their own time.

Understanding the impermanent nature of emotions can provide reassurance when a wave of anger, anxiety, or depression hits. Knowing that the emotion will pass, we are better able to stay calm as we observe these uncomfortable sensations rise and fall.

We Don't Need to Fix; Observing is Enough

It may feel like a waste of time to sit back and observe since the thinking mind is continually trying to fix any given situation. The thinking mind will often create a sense of restlessness to distract us from experiencing the emotion.

It's important to remember that we don't have to solve a given problem for our emotional state to shift. This is particularly important to remember when the problem at hand is unsolvable—such as the loss of a loved one or living with stage four cancer. In these circumstances, it is essential to trust that simply the act of observing our thoughts and emotions is *enough* to reduce the stress—we don't have to *solve* the problem to experience some relief. By repeating the Observe practice on a daily basis, we create new neural pathways to be able to relate to our difficult circumstances with more ease and grace.

For example, when I meditated during the five months of chemotherapy, nothing had changed on the situational level—I still had cancer in my body. But when I observed my emotions without judgment, I dropped into the present moment, and I experienced peace. With mindfulness, I changed the way I related to the cancer and I became liberated from the grip of my painful emotions.

The Three Options

When a challenging emotion arises, we have three options. First, we can be *in* the emotion and let it take over the psyche, such as anger spiraling into rage, fear into panic, or sadness into depression. The second option is to repress or distract ourselves from feeling the emotion by numbing ourselves with television, food, alcohol, drugs, or staying overly busy with work. Many people cope with their emotions in one of these two ways, but neither option is a healthy way to process them.

Mindfulness offers a third option—*observe the emotion*. We can learn to observe our feelings without being overly expressive or repressive.

It may feel overwhelming to simply observe and allow intense emotions to rise in the body without containment. But a mindfulness tool, such as the LOVEE Method, creates a safe container in which the emotion can be expressed, processed, and integrated.

During my cancer treatment, when a strong emotion welled up, I recognized that I had the choice regarding how to manage it. I could curl up into the fetal position and cry, I could turn on the television and distract myself, or I could take a seat on my meditation cushion.

Although I caved into my emotions and chose options one and two quite often, I reminded myself that the most self-loving and self-healing choice was always option number three. I realized that cancer would either define me, destroy me, or empower me. And, I always had the choice.

The Goal of Mindfulness

Although we associate meditation with calming the mind, it is essential to remember that the purpose of mindfulness is to acknowledge whatever is present without judgment or reactivity. The goal of mindfulness is not to make the anger go away, rather it is to cultivate a nonreactive mindset.

Sometimes challenging emotions disappear during mindfulness

practice, but this isn't always the case. It's important not to fall into the trap of meditating *in order to* settle the mind or make an emotion disappear, as sometimes this doesn't happen and then we feel like a failure. The key is to observe the emotion without an attachment about how we will feel at the end of practice.

So rather than meditating in order to calm our thinking mind, we can choose to meditate with the intentions of expanding our awareness (the observing mind), as well as cultivating a balanced nervous system.

The Physiology of Mindfulness

We can also meditate for our health, both mental and physical. When we practice mindfulness, studies show that brain activity shifts toward patterns related to calm and focused attention.[1] Since we are cultivating mental states of wellbeing, feelings of anxiety and depression subsequently decrease, and often our relationships improve.

The good news is these mental states can be long-lasting because mindfulness affects neuroplasticity, which is the ability for neurons to move in the brain and form new connections. Due to the neuroplastic ability of the brain, we can learn something new, practice the skill over and over again, and eventually become an expert. Whenever we practice a new skill, our neurons shift and create new connections in the brain.[2]

Practicing mindfulness is no different. When we establish a daily practice, our neurons shift and create new mental patterns leading to more calm and focus in our inner experience.

The structure of the brain itself also changes with mindfulness. Studies show that the gray matter (the tissue containing neurons) of meditators is thicker in certain brain regions compared to nonmeditators.[3]

There is a growing body of research that demonstrates that mindfulness has a positive effect on our physical health, as well. Multiple studies show that mindfulness strengthens the immune system by increasing the number of cells that fight infection.[4]

It's crucial to keep the immune system as strong as possible during cancer treatment to avoid secondary infections as well as after treatment to help prevent recurrence. Therefore, we can add mindfulness practice to our daily list of immune-boosting activities, along with a healthy diet and exercise.

Professor Jon Kabat-Zinn developed the Mindfulness-Based Stress Reduction (MBSR) program in the 1970s, and has been at the forefront of mindfulness research related to medical health.

Having a goal to integrate mindfulness into medicine, Kabat-Zinn has conducted numerous studies that found that his 8-week MBSR program benefitted various medical groups, including improvements in immune function and psychological health in women with breast cancer.[5]

Don't Believe Everything You Think

With enough mindfulness practice, we get to know the observing mind and begin to understand what it feels like to view our lives from this neutral point of view as opposed to the reactive thinking mind.

Identifying with the observing mind, rather than the thinking mind, liberates us from the rollercoaster of our thoughts. When we realize that the voice in our heads is not who we are, and we simply observe this voice without trying to change anything, we gain perspective and become free from the suffering created by the thinking mind.

In the book *The Power of Now*, global spiritual teacher Eckhart Tolle says that we activate a higher level of consciousness when we take the seat of the observer. Tolle says, "The beginning of freedom is the realization that you are not 'the thinker.' You begin to realize that there is a vast realm of intelligence beyond thought, that thought is only a tiny aspect of that intelligence. You also realize that all the things that truly matter—beauty, love, creativity, joy, inner peace—arise from beyond the mind. You begin to awaken."

The Observe Practice Meditation

> Listen to the meditation online at:
> **www.meditationforbreastcancer.com**

    Let's begin by gently closing your eyes or lowering your gaze to the floor. Sitting up tall and relaxing your shoulders down your back. Allowing your hands to rest gently on your lap. Making any small adjustments to your body so that you feel comfortable. Take a few deep breaths, in and out through the nose, allowing your body to soften.

    Bringing your attention to the breath flowing in and out of the abdomen. Notice the abdomen expand on the inhale and contract on the exhale. Let the breath be natural, noticing the gentle expansion and contraction at the abdomen. Noticing the gentle wave of breath. The breath flows in, abdomen expands, the breath flows out, the abdomen contracts.

    Establishing your abdomen as your anchor, a place of comfort, a place of refuge, that brings your nervous system into a state of ease.

    Now bring your attention to other sensations in the body. Emotions such as anxiety, anger, or sadness sometimes create sensations in the body, such as contraction in the gut, tension in the shoulders, or heaviness in the hips. Like moving a flashlight throughout the body from head to toe, try and locate these emotions by scanning the entire body for sensation.

    Don't worry if you don't feel anything. Sensing emotions in the body is difficult for most people at first. But with practice, you should begin to feel subtle sensations. So let's give it a try.

    Take a couple more breaths and drop deeper into the body. Let's focus our flashlight in the abdominal area. Are there any sensations here? Any soreness in the hips, or clenching in the stomach? We don't have to create anything, just notice whatever is here.

Remember that you don't need to try and change any of the sensations, just observe them. The purpose of this practice is not to change a sensation or make it go away, it is to enhance the observer consciousness. The purpose of this practice is to make the flashlight brighter.

If you find a strong sensation, focus on it for a few seconds and notice what happens. The sensation may increase, decrease, or dissolve altogether. It may change into another sensation, move to another part of the body, or it may stay the same. The key is not to be attached to what the emotion does. We are simply observing it without trying to change anything.

You might say to the sensation, "You are welcome here, you can stay as long as you need. I'm just witnessing anything you'd like to do." If the emotions or the sensations start to feel overwhelming at any time, you can always return to your anchor, back to the gentle wave of breath at the abdomen.

Next, let's bring the flashlight up to the chest area, scanning the chest and upper back for any notable sensations. Notice the breath causing the chest to rise and fall. Notice your heart beating. Notice the subtle movements of your vertebrae and back muscles as you breath.

Now observe any sensations in this entire area. Is there tightness in the shoulders, soreness in the back? Rather than judging, bring some curiosity to the sensations. You might think, "Hmm, the tingling in my back is interesting, I wonder what it will do next." Continuing to scan throughout the torso, bringing your attention, openness, and curiosity to any sensations you discover.

Now gently bring your attention to the areas of the neck, head, and face. Are there any sensations here? Continue to observe the sensations without judgment, with openness and curiosity.

Again, if you find a strong sensation, I invite you to focus on it for a few seconds and notice what happens. Remember we are just observing and letting it be. You can say to the sensation, "You are welcome here, you can stay as long as you'd like." And if the sensation ever becomes too strong, shift your attention back to your anchor, back to a place of safety and comfort.

In these last couple minutes of our meditation, I invite you to bring your focus to the strongest sensation in your body, whether it was in the hips, back, or shoulders, bring your full attention to it. Continuing to track the sensation with openness and curiosity, simply observing the subtle movements of the sensation, back and forth, stronger and weaker. Allowing the sensation to be there. Breathe into the knowing that we don't need to fix or change the sensation; all we need to do is observe it.

Now slowly expanding your awareness to sense your entire body. How is your body feeling? How is your mind? If you're not feeling relaxed and calm, that is perfectly okay. The purpose of this practice is to get to know our Observer consciousness, it's about brightening the flashlight, it's about experiencing the sensations in our bodies without judgment and instead with a sense of curiosity and ease.

By learning to observe and be nonreactive with sensations in the body, we are learning to observe and be nonreactive with whatever happens in our lives.

Now let's begin to bring the meditation to a close. Feeling your feet on the floor. Feeling your legs on the chair or cushion. Feeling your hands on your lap. And, whenever you're ready, end the meditation and gently open your eyes.

Part 3
"V" *is for* Value

Chapter 7
Going into the Fire

"What matters most is how well you walk through the fire."
Charles Bukowksi, poet

Ninja-Mindset Training

In preparation for my first chemo, I applied my corporate-America experience to become the CEO of my own health. I created an outline of tasks for my post-chemo week of recovery. I mapped out the exact day and time I would take each pharmaceutical. If a particular side effect occurred, I knew which medication to take and which meditation to practice. I was not going to miss a beat. I focused on my health and wellness as if my life depended on it—because it did.

My mind was extremely fragile, so I created a plan to cultivate a mindset of strength to help me cope. I named my mental training: "Project Ninja-Mindset", which had three main steps:

1. Protect My Mind
   - Do not consume news or social media that leads to depression or anxiety. Only watch feel-good movies and listen to uplifting music that brings me joy.
   - Do not listen to other people's negative stories about cancer that can fuel fearful, worst-case-scenario thinking. Only participate with support circles and social media groups that promote optimism and positivity.

2. Prioritize Self-Care
   - Learn how to love and take care of my mind and body.
   - Take a walk in nature every day and practice being present. Stop and smell the flowers, notice intricate patterns on trees, and pet every dog that crosses my path.
3. Cultivate Gratitude
   - Make eye contact and say "thank you" to every nurse and doctor I encounter. Savor the feeling of gratitude for their life-saving work.
   - At the end of each day, write down three things I am grateful for.

"Project Ninja-Mindset" also included reading these empowering messages that I posted on a large whiteboard in my bedroom:

- I am taking care of my health with gentleness and love.
- I am sailing through these treatments with courage, joy, grace, surrender, and gratitude.
- I am a radiant Spirit having a human experience.
- The medicine is healing me and not harming my healthy cells.
- I surrender, relax, and receive.
- I am at ease and use my mindfulness tools to experience peace.
- I trust that everything is unfolding for my highest good.
- All is well.
- I'VE GOT THIS!

These affirmations served as constant reminders that I could choose my thoughts at any time. Whenever my mind spiraled down the rabbit hole of victim consciousness, I would stop myself, read the whiteboard, and get back on track with my commitment to staying strong, empowered, and peaceful throughout this journey.

Needless to say, I was reading these messages several times a day. It took a lot of effort to stay positive and not let my mind wander into despair. So much effort that I could almost feel the neurons in my brain rewiring from mental habits of victimhood to new patterns of ease, strength, and power.

The Journey Officially Begins

Before receiving chemotherapy, I first had to have a port-a-cath, or "port," surgically inserted into my chest. Since chemo could potentially damage my blood vessels, the port provided a safe interface between my body and the harsh medicine. I had to come to terms with the fact that this square-inch plastic box, inserted just under my skin and over my heart, would take residence in my chest for the next five months.

The night before my port surgery, I was hyper-focused on my ninja-mindset training as if I were going into battle. I read the empowering messages on my whiteboard over and over again.

I was ready.

The next morning, I arrived at the UCLA surgical center. The second I walked into the building, my ninja-mindset went out the window. Since I had no physical symptoms, cancer had only been a mental concept up until that point. But since I would feel and see this port protruding from under my skin, it served as physical proof that having cancer was, indeed, my reality.

A nurse brought me into the exam room and a tsunami of fear welled up inside of me.

I was not ready.

An hour before surgery, I laid on the hospital bed answering my nurse's pre-op questions. Every cell in my body was screaming in defiance. Getting the port meant I could not turn back—I was on the path of chemo. *This is really happening! No, no! I don't want this!*

In the middle of answering one of the nurse's questions, a wave of panic completely engulfed me—my breath quickened, I hyperventilated, and I passed out. It was my first panic attack.

I regained consciousness with an oxygen mask over my mouth and several nurses around my bed looking down at me. The doctor walked up to the right side of my bed.

"Hi, Sharon. I'll be doing the surgery today, and I wanted to stop by and say hello," he said. "Don't worry, I do four of these a day. It'll only take about forty-five minutes. It's all going to be okay."

I nodded my head. His words and demeanor were reassuring. Our eyes locked for a brief moment and I immediately trusted him. Then he dashed off to reassure another patient.

A moment later, the anesthetic began to kick in and the wheels of my hospital bed started to turn. It was time.

About an hour later, I woke up with a plastic device embedded in my chest, just above my heart. With quiet tears, I put my hand over my heart, closed my eyes, and took a deep breath.

This was no longer a bad dream. The port brought the mental concept of having cancer into the physical realm. This surgery represented the first step in the long, hard road to recovery.

Getting on the Train

To wrap my head around this year of treatments, I likened it to a train ride with the following "stops":

1. Minor Surgery inserting the Port-a-Cath (the first stop was done!)
2. Six Chemotherapy Infusions (with challenging side effects)
3. Mastectomy and Reconstruction Surgeries (both on the same day)
4. Twenty Radiation Treatments (over the course of a month)
5. Minor Surgery to create a new Nipple
6. The Nipple Tattoo
7. Eleven additional Chemotherapy Infusions (which had minimal side effects) every three weeks until the one-year mark

I knew I had a choice regarding how I would begin this tumultuous journey. Either I would be dragged behind this train kicking and screaming and resisting every stop along the way, or I could step aboard the train with dignity and find a comfortable seat. I was typically a "doer" in life, but it was time for me to let go of control and simply allow the UCLA medical team to take care of me.

Celebrating the completion of my first five months of treatments.

Going into the Fire

My first chemotherapy session was May 30, 2018. That morning, I triple-checked my "chemo bag" to make sure I was prepared. The bag was complete with a neck pillow, an electric blanket, my iTunes synced to my meditations, and frozen gloves and booties. I read that freezing my hands and feet prevented neuropathy, a condition where fingers and toes lose sensation due to peripheral nerve damage. Freezing my hands and feet reduced circulation and therefore decreased the chances of the chemo to reach the tips of my fingers and toes.

By the same logic, I would wear ice packs on my head, or "cold caps," throughout the chemo treatment to reduce hair loss. The ice packs would be swapped out every thirty minutes to make sure my scalp stayed frozen, which inhibited circulation of the chemo to my scalp's hair follicles.

At 9:00 a.m., Mom and I walked into the infusion room and a nurse greeted us with a kind smile.

"Welcome, Sharon," the nurse said. "You can sit anywhere you'd like."

The infusion room was surprisingly relaxing, with floor-to-ceiling windows allowing sunlight to fill the space. Mom and I sat down in the far corner, which offered a view of the Santa Monica Mountains.

Mom placed the first cold cap onto my head and strapped it down. The cold cap sent searing pain through my scalp, similar to an ice-cream headache but from the outside—and without the ice-cream.

"Ahhh, that's cold," I said, taking deep breaths. "Ohhh, ouch." I reminded myself that the pain would stop once the scalp went numb. Sitting in that intense pain, I thought to myself, *Maybe losing my hair wouldn't be so bad? What is worse: going bald or enduring this pain every treatment?*

Debating between those two evils was agonizing. Luckily, my scalp went numb before I decided. That was my cue to slip on the frozen gloves and booties to, once again, endure the painful numbing process.

The nurse wheeled over a steel infusion stand that held a clear, plastic bag containing my first chemical infusion.

There it is, I thought, looking at the bag of liquid. *The clear poison that will save my life.*

"Hi Sharon, how are you doing?" said the nurse, Ruby, offering a sweet smile.

"I'm doing okay," I said, wearing my helmet-shaped cold cap. "I'm scared … and cold."

"Well, you're in good hands here," Ruby said. "This needle will hurt just for a second." She pricked the port in my chest with the infusion needle, which was attached to a long clear tube connected to the bag of liquid chemotherapy.

I watched the first drop of chemo flow into my bloodstream, and my entire body cringed with goosebumps. As a yoga and meditation teacher, I prided myself on being pharmaceutical-free, and I fiercely resisted the idea of infusing such toxic chemicals into my body. But I also had a dear friend with breast cancer who took the all-natural route and refused chemotherapy and surgery. Although she lived with cancer for five years, cancer took her life only six months ago, and I was still grieving the loss of my friend.

With that, I took a deep breath and reframed the situation. I looked at the clear bag of chemicals and said, "Thank you for saving my life." With each drop of chemo in my system, I was one step closer to being recovered.

The LOVEE Method

With my chemotherapy nurse, Ruby, UCLA Health.

I realized that willingly allowing someone to put poison into my body was the most courageous act of trust I had ever done. Similar to my experience on the beach, this profound level of surrender led to a feeling of deep peace.

I placed earbuds into my ears and began listening to a meditation. I visualized the chemicals as healing rainbows pouring into my bloodstream. I greeted the chemo, not as a foreign invader, but as a welcomed savior.

While sitting in the infusion chair, I thought to myself, *Thank you, chemo. Thank you for healing me. You are welcome here. Thank you for your intelligence to find and dissolve malignant cells while leaving healthy cells unharmed. I am so grateful for you. Thank you for saving my life.*

These phrases were hard to say at first since I had so much resistance, but I was committed to cultivating gratitude and staying positive throughout this challenging day, so I continued the practice.

After about an hour of listening to meditations, my mind let go of all resistance and my body melted into the infusion chair. The cocktail of drugs streaming through the IV also made me drowsy, and I fell asleep for a couple of hours.

I woke up around noon. I blinked my eyes open and my dear friend Kirsten had arrived.

"Hi Sharon, how are you feeling?" Kirsten asked. "I brought you some homemade broth."

"Oh, hi. Thank you so much for coming," I said with a smile. "Thank you for the broth, that's so nice of you."

"Of course, I'm happy to help," she said and took a seat. For the next few hours, Kirsten helped Mom swap out the cold caps every thirty minutes. Kirsten was also a Reiki practitioner and she offered blessings onto the bags of chemo. Even though we didn't talk much, it was comforting to know that my friend was there, by my side.

Kirsten offering Reiki during chemotherapy.

At 3:00 p.m., I had to get out of my chair to go to the bathroom, which was an ordeal. I made sure there weren't any tubes caught on anything and then I stood up and walked gingerly, wheeling the IV stand along with me.

On the walk back, I met eyes with another woman going through chemo. She had not lost her hair yet, so I knew it was one of her first sessions.

"Hello," I said with a smile. "What's your name?"

"Hi there," she said. "My name is Linda."

"Hi, Linda, I'm Sharon," I said. "This is my first session, the first of six. How about you?"

"It's mine, too," she said with a smile. "And, I'm also getting six, so we're on the same track."

"Well, I'm sorry you're going through this," I said, "but I'm glad we're going through it together."

"You're my chemo buddy," she said. "I'll see you in three weeks."

I gave her smile, then returned to my station. Kirsten was playing music on her iPhone and we spontaneously started dancing in the infusion room. With my frozen helmet, gloves, and booties, I was not the most fluid dancer, but I could definitely nail the "robot" move.

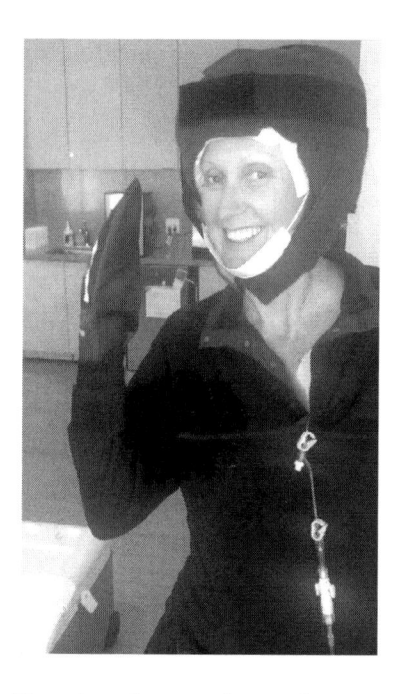

Dancing during chemotherapy.

It was 4:00 p.m. and we had one more hour to go in this eight-hour marathon. The mini-dance party wiped me out, and I fell asleep for the last hour.

"Wake up, Sharon," said Mom, taking off the final cold cap. "You're all done. It's time to go home now."

Chemotherapy Meditation

Practice while Receiving Chemotherapy

Listen to the meditation online at:
www.meditationforbreastcancer.com

I first want to say that I'm so sorry for what you're going through. I've been there. I know the feeling you're having right now. This is a hard time and you're not alone. May this meditation serve as a caring friend to hold your hand through this day. May this meditation serve to bring your mind into a gentle state of surrender, and your body into a relaxed state of ease. May this meditation create a peaceful inner experience, releasing any and all resistance, and calling upon the natural healing intelligence of the body.

As you take a seat in the infusion chair, gently close your eyes, take a few deep breaths, and allow your body to soften. Feel the contact between you and the chair beneath you. Feel the support under your back, your shoulders, and your head. Feel the support of the chair under your hips and under your legs. Take an inhale, and on the exhale, allow your body to surrender and completely melt into the chair. Feel the entire body fully supported and held.

Bring one hand to your abdomen and take a few deep, slow breaths. Expanding the stomach on the inhale and gently contracting on the exhale. Focusing on the sensation of the abdomen expanding and contracting. Focus on the breath gently flowing in and flowing out.

Slightly open your eyes and see the beautiful humans, angels in the flesh, that are all around you, here to support you, nurture you, and care for you. Trust that you are right where you're supposed to be, you're in great hands and in great care. All you have to do is relax and let the doctors and nurses do their jobs. Your body feels comfortable and calm. When you're ready, gently close your eyes, knowing that you're in a safe place, you are well nurtured, and cared for.

With each inhale, imagine that you're filling your body with light, love, and grace. With each exhale, you're releasing and letting go of any resistance or tightness in the body. On the inhale, visualize your cells being nourished in healing light; on the exhale, relax the body fully and completely. With each breath, allow yourself to feel even more relaxed.

As the medicine enters your body, take deep, slow breaths and imagine it as healing nectar. This medicine is filled with intelligence, care, and blessings, and is designed just for you, for your optimal healing. Allow yourself to receive this medicine fully; it may feel cold or uncomfortable but it is safe, it is good, it is the right thing to do for your healing.

Continuing to breathe deeply, carried on the breath is beautiful healing light. This life force energy washes through your body with each inhale and exhale. Feeling luminous golden light nourishing your body from the top of your head, down the torso and arms, into the chest, abdomen and pelvis, down into the legs and feet. From head to toe, this beautiful golden light blesses your entire body.

This divine light welcomes the medicine into the body, guides it to the malignant cells to dissolve them, then escorts the medicine out of the body while leaving healthy cells unharmed. If the medicine affects any healthy cells, the golden light instantly regenerates them.

With each breath, you are creating more and more of this golden light, which is the natural healing intelligence of the body. Continue the visualization of the medicine escorted by the golden light traveling through the body, identifying and dissolving malignant cells. Visualize cancer cells dissolving gently, effortlessly, and completely. Continuing this visualization throughout your treatment today, remembering that you are deeply loved and cared for every step of the way.

You are moving through this time with great ease, great strength, and great love. Visualize yourself on the other side of these treatments with radiant, vibrant health. Let yourself find a gentle smile as you offer thanks for the medicine that is bringing you one step closer to this vision.

There are so many gifts and blessings to be grateful for: gratitude for the health care team, for the healing medicine, for the natural healing intelligence of the body, as well as gratitude for the precious gift of life. This moment offers an opportunity to cultivate deep peace and gratitude at every layer of your being: your mind, your body, your breath, and your Spirit.

The radiant golden light of gratitude surrounds you now. You are nurtured and held in this beautiful light of wellbeing. All you have to do is relax in this sphere of appreciation and let the medicine work its healing magic.

Rest easy, beautiful one. Trust. Continuing to feel the golden light of gratitude and peace. Place one hand on your heart. From my heart to yours, I'm sending you so much love and peace. I love you. I honor you. I cherish you. You are me, and I am you. All is well, sweetheart. All is well. All is well.

Chapter 8
I'm Only Human

"Be kind whenever possible. It is always possible."
The 14th Dalai Lama

Hot Chocolate

The sun was setting and my first chemotherapy session was complete. As Mom drove me home from the infusion center, she asked me how it went.

"It's not so bad," I said. "Strangely enough, the hardest part was the cold caps. But the infusions didn't hurt, and everyone was really nice. Let's hope the side effects aren't too terrible."

When I got home, I received a text from Will.

"Hey, Sharon, how did your treatment go today?" read the text.

"Hey, honey. Everything went well. Thanks for checking in <3," I texted back.

"Of course. Just letting you know that I'm thinking of you," he texted.

"Thank you, love. I'm doing good, just really tired. Heading to sleep now. Sweet dreams," I texted back.

In my dreams, I was standing on a platform and a train stopped in front of me. The chemo-train had arrived!

The train door slid open, and my surgeon, Dr. Kusske, flashed her radiant smile and reached out her hand.

"Come on board, Sharon," she said. "We're happy you're here!"

I took her hand and stepped onto the train. I looked around and saw other patients that had been with me in the infusion room that day. I found a comfortable window seat, reclined my chair, and the wheels of the train began to move.

My oncologist, Dr. McCann, walked up to my seat and offered me a drink. "Hi, Sharon, it's wonderful to see you. Here's a special cocktail I made just for you!"

"A cocktail?" I said with a smile, thinking it was a gin-and-tonic. "Why, thank you!"

I brought the glass to my lips and realized it was not the kind of cocktail I was used to, rather it was a "chemo cocktail." I quickly put the drink down into my chair's cup holder. *I'll just put this down right here.*

Suddenly, I saw all of my nurses and doctors singing and doing cartwheels in the aisles of the train, reminiscent of the "hot chocolate" scene in the movie *The Polar Express*.

While traveling along a steep mountain, the train began to pick up speed. As the train took a sharp turn, the wheels spun off the track and the train catapulted toward the valley below.

I woke up in a panic. I shook my head and took a breath. It was only a dream. I typically didn't have such vivid dreams, so I assumed it was a reaction to all of the chemicals in my system.

It was 4:00 a.m., and I couldn't fall back asleep. Lying in bed, I looked around my room and noticed that the crown molding needed a coat of paint.

Wide awake and restless, I jumped out of bed, stirred up a gallon of flat white, and started painting. Once I finished painting the crown molding in my bedroom, I moved to the kitchen, then the dining room, then the living room, and then the bathroom. Then, I circled back and painted every door in the house white.

At 4:00 p.m., after twelve hours of painting, my roommate Shalini came home and found me on a ladder painting the hallway ceiling.

"Hey Shalini, do you want me to paint the crown molding in your bedroom?" I asked.

"Sure," she said, giving me a quizzical look, knowing that I had received chemo the day before. "Sharon, how are you doing this?"

I stopped and thought for a moment. "Oh my God, steroids were part of my chemo!" I said. "Whoa. It's time for me to put the brush down."

I slowly climbed down the ladder. With a big smile, my roommate hugged me, and we had a good laugh.

"Want to go to a restorative yoga class with me?" she asked, clearly seeing my need to calm down. "My friend can pick us up in twenty minutes."

"That sounds great," I said.

During the yoga class, my body started to feel heavy and achy, similar to having the flu. I laid down on my back and placed one hand on my heart and the other hand on my belly. The side effects were kicking in and it was once again time to take out my ninja-mindset toolbox.

With several breaths, I imagined filling my body with love and positive energy, along with gratitude for the chemo, my medical team, and my supportive friends.

After class, my roommate decided to stay at the studio, but her friend offered to give me a ride home. As we were sitting in traffic, we heard a beeping noise.

"Do you have your seatbelt on?" he asked.

"Yeah, I do," I replied. "What's that beeping?"

"I don't know," he said while looking at the dashboard. "This is a new car, so I'm not sure."

We were both looking around, then he stared right at me and said, "The beeping is coming from you."

He had a startled and curious look on his face, as if I were wearing a bomb.

"Oh!" I said. "It's okay, it's coming from this patch on my arm." I showed him the patch on my left shoulder. "I didn't want to say anything, but I have breast cancer, and I got my first chemo yesterday. This patch has medicine that gets injected twenty-four hours later. I guess the beeping means the drug is going in now. Sorry to alarm you!"

Although I was embarrassed to reveal that I had cancer, he didn't seem to mind. He gave me a look of relief about the beeping combined with compassion for the reason. Once we arrived at my house, he parked the car and gave me a big hug.

"You're going to be alright," he said, looking me straight in the eyes. "I will pray for you."

"Thank you," I said with tears welling up. "Thank you so much."

I walked into my bedroom and laid down on my bed. I could feel the medicine from the patch moving into my bloodstream. The drug was called Neulasta, which boosted my immune system by stimulating bone marrow to make more white blood cells. Chemotherapy compromises the immune system, so it was crucial to take Neulasta twenty-four hours later to stave off secondary infections.

Neulasta had a stinging sensation as it moved through my body. Fear began to creep in. *This doesn't feel good. What is this medicine going to do to me?* It streamed for forty-five minutes, and once it hit my brain, I fell into a deep sleep.

Here Come the Side Effects

For the next two days, I was on an E-ticket ride at Disneyland, but more like a scary version of Disney, on LSD. Colors were brighter, sounds were distorted, and my taste buds were off-kilter.

Two days after chemo, I walked into the kitchen and made myself some oatmeal. "Does this taste weird to you?" I asked my roommate, Jared, offering him a bite. "My taste buds are a bit funky, so I can't tell if things have gone bad."

"You're saying you've got funky buds?" he said, which made us both laugh.

He took a bite and said, "Tastes fine to me."

"Well, I don't want it. I feel nauseous anyway. You can have it," I said, making a sour face.

"Why does the chemo affect your taste buds?" he said, in between scoops.

"Well, cancer cells replicate faster than most cells in the body, and chemo targets not only cancer but *any* cell that replicates quickly," I said, putting on my teacher hat. "You know when you bite your tongue and it heals instantly? That's because the cells on your tongue replicate really fast."

"Oh, interesting," he said, adding cinnamon to the oatmeal.

"Yeah, it's the same for the gut and the skin, so I'm sure I'll have side effects in those places, too," I said, disheartened by what was soon to come.

"I'm so sorry," he said. "That's no fun."

"Yeah, I have a metallic taste in my mouth. It feels like I'm chewing on metal," I said. "Are you sure there aren't staples in that oatmeal?"

"Nope, no staples here," he said with a smile, followed by taking the last bite. "Well, let me know when you have funky buds again. I'm happy to support you."

"I will," I said with a laugh.

That afternoon, Mom came over and we went for a walk on the Venice Canals. She put a big sun hat on my head and reminded me that my skin would be extra sensitive.

As we walked, the Neulasta caused sharp pain in the bones of my legs that felt like fireworks. To associate the pain with gratitude, whenever I felt a blast, I visualized white blood cells being created to fend off infection.

Ooo, ouch! Thank you fireworks in my bones. Thank you for boosting my immune system. Ouch! Thank you.

Along with being foggy-headed, the combination of the chemo and Neulasta made me a bit wobbly, and I reached for Mom's arm for stability. My reality was altered, everything around me was extra vibrant, and any sense of logic was thrown out the window.

"Look at this gorgeous turquoise flower!" I said to Mom, pointing to a purple Morning Glory. Mom gave me a perplexed look and tried not to laugh. Instead of saying a word, she held my arm and guided her drugged-up daughter along the next canal.

The Courage of a Lioness

The next day was not nearly as fun. I woke up at 3:00 a.m. buckled over in abdominal pain. The chemo had hit my gut and it felt like a knife was searing through my intestines. My fear about the pain compounded the physical misery. *Is this a complication? Do I have to go to the hospital?*

Many of my friends had called me a warrior for going through chemotherapy, but lying there curled up on my bed, I felt anything but brave. I realized that my first lesson I'd have to learn on this journey was—*courage*.

After ten minutes of crying in the fetal position, I asked myself, *How can I be stronger than this pain? How can I be courageous right now? What does courage even look like?*

Wait, I know.

I forced myself off the bed, sat down on my meditation pillow, and closed my eyes.

"*This* is what courage looks like," I said to myself, shaking, with the determination of a rock alchemizing into crystal.

While in meditation, I brought my attention to my fear and noticed that it was making the physical pain worse. Recalling "The Second Arrow" parable taught at the meditation retreat, I realized that by being fearful I was throwing the second arrow. This awareness dissolved the fear and I began to observe the painful sensations in my gut. By the end of the twenty-minute meditation, the physical pain lessened and I felt a sense of peace.

I discovered the definition of courage, right then and there. Rather than distract myself from the pain, I mustered the courage to *sit* with it. It would have been much easier to continue crying on my bed or distract myself with television or social media. It took *courage,* however, to get on my meditation cushion and observe the pain directly.

I began to trust that my daily practice was taking me to a place of great fortitude. I was lifting the weights of mindfulness and I was getting stronger.

To face chemo, I had to cultivate an immense amount of courage.

Becoming a Scientist of my Own Mind

Even though I was meditating with the intention of managing my emotions, I experienced another unexpected benefit—I became more aware of my mental, emotional, and behavioral patterns. I became a scientist of my own mind and I adopted a curious attitude about the data I was collecting.

Just like a scientist, I didn't judge my findings, I simply took note and continued my experiment of self-discovery. My mind was the laboratory for inner exploration, and mindfulness was the microscope that brought my patterns into focus. I realized that my personality was merely an amalgamation of likes and dislikes, mental and emotional patterns, and how I reacted in various situations.

From the observer perspective, I was able to understand how my current patterns had been created through hardships in my childhood. I also became aware that my sense of self was not a fixed, solid identity, but a fluid, energetic experience that was constantly moving. Perhaps this idea of "self" is more of a verb than a noun—always changing and always in motion.

Ever since diagnosis I was meditating every day. And over time, I began to see repeated patterns, such as the need for approval, need for protection, as well as a need to be "right." One night, deep in meditation, I had a breakthrough: *What*, exactly, was seeking approval? *What* needed protection? *What* was trying to prove or defend itself? *What* needed to be right? When my mind dropped deep enough to see beneath the patterns, I found that nothing was there.

One of the gifts of having a near-death experience is awakening to the truth that the ego is an illusion. There is nothing to prove, seek, or defend. I realized that these thought patterns had been creating daily suffering for myself and others my entire life—*for no good reason.*

With this new awareness, pieces of my ego broke apart like a jigsaw puzzle and then dissolved. The veil of my egoic patterns had been lifted, I felt immense freedom, and I was one step closer to understanding the true nature of reality.

Chapter 9

The Value Practice—Value the Emotion

*"When you arise in the morning, think of
what a precious privilege it is to be alive—
to breathe, to think, to enjoy, to love."*
Marcus Aurelius, Roman emperor

We Are All in This Together

In 2018, I was among the 263,694 women diagnosed with breast cancer in the US. I learned that 1 in 8 US women (about 12 percent) will develop invasive breast cancer over the course of her lifetime.[1]

Although it was a terrible circumstance, at least I knew that I was not alone. I was connected not only to those with cancer but with everyone experiencing suffering, and I felt closer to humanity than ever before.

In his song "One Love," Bob Marley proclaimed that we all share the same love. By the same token, I believe that we also share the same pain, which is equally beautiful. The fact that everyone experiences challenging times is what brings us together.

Even though the level of pain is different in various circumstances, the fundamental experience of human suffering (just like love) is the same and we are collectively in a healing process.

To connect with other women going through breast cancer treatment, I attended support groups offered by UCLA. I believe that human connection is fundamental to both emotional and physical health. People who have strong relationships are not as frightened by difficult circumstances and are better able to cope. Studies show that women with breast cancer who attend support groups experience less anxiety.[2]

After sharing in the support group, I felt understood, which was incredibly healing. I didn't need to isolate myself during this challenging time. Knowing that I was not alone provided courage, since I drew on the collective strength of all the other women traveling along this journey with me.

Improving our Self-Awareness

When we are in inquiry with our emotions as opposed to resistance, we also improve our self-awareness, which is the ability to recognize and understand our own emotions. In order to grow and evolve, we must turn inward, recognize and acknowledge our emotional patterns in order to learn where we are stuck, what is important to us, and how to improve our relationships.

During the Value practice, we acknowledge that our emotions are a natural part of the human condition. We value all of our emotions equally—from a mindfulness perspective, happiness is not any better or worse than anger as both emotions are simply energies that come and go in our experience.

It's natural to feel judgmental, anxious, angry, or sad throughout the day. But problems occur when we create a "lens" through which we perceive and interpret our lives. For example, if we create a lens of disgust, we can become chronically judgmental of ourselves and others. We can also create lenses of anxiety, anger, or depression, interpreting the world through these "negative" emotions.

Mindfulness helps us clean these lenses of perception so that we see things more clearly and accurately. We are able to release stories from the past, let go of resentments, and simply enjoy the present moment. When we are fully present, we have a more vibrant life experience—the grass is greener, the sky is bluer, and the roses are more fragrant since mindfulness improves the *quality* of our attention.

With a daily mindfulness practice, we become more aware of our emotional and behavioral patterns such as victimhood, defensiveness, or hyper-vigilance. By shining the light of mindfulness onto these patterns, they slowly begin to dissolve, making this practice a journey of coming home to the most authentic version of ourselves.

Our Emotions are Here to Tell Us Something

The Value practice helps us to reframe our emotions from something negative to something helpful. We create a different relationship with our anxiety, anger, and depression. We befriend these emotions rather than push them away or judge ourselves for having them.

Along with valuing these "negative" emotions for connecting us to others and increasing our self-awareness, we also can value them because they are here to tell us something. For example, anger reveals what really matters to us, including our boundaries and principles, and prompts us into action against injustice. Jealousy brings to light what we really desire in life. Fear tells us that we feel unsafe and need to protect ourselves. Anxiety alerts us that we are out of balance in some way. Sadness informs us that we really care about something that we've lost or has changed, or never received. It is the release of sadness, such as the healing process of crying, that allows us to let go and move forward.

With a sense of openness and curiosity, we can ask our emotions, *Why are you here? What do you need to tell me?* Specifically, if the emotion is anger, we can ask, *What boundaries have been crossed?* If it is fear or anxiety, we can ask, *How can I change my environment so that I feel safe? How can I bring my nervous system back into balance?* If the emotion is sadness, we can ask, *What do I need to let go of?*

Also, since emotions are simply energies in motion, there's the possibility that we have absorbed the emotion from another person or from the collective. So, we can also ask the emotion, *Is this energy mine or does it belong to someone else?* If we sense that the emotion originated elsewhere, we can send the energy back to where it came from. But if the emotion stemmed from our own patterns, we can simply continue with the LOVEE practice.

With the Value practice, we create a more welcoming relationship with our anxiety, anger, and depression. Our emotions become our allies—we trust them, we work with them, and we allow them to inform our choices in life.

Quieting the Inner Critic

We can also value our emotions by acknowledging that they are essential for our survival. Our "negative" emotions—such as disgust, fear, anger, and sadness—all have critical roles in keeping the human species alive, therefore we mustn't judge ourselves when we feel them. By understanding the evolutionary functions of these emotions, we are able to recognize them as valuable parts of our human experience.

First, let's take a deeper look at the emotion of disgust, or judgment. Many people experience disgust toward themselves in the form of the "inner critic." Professor and author, Brené Brown, says that feeling shame, or disgust toward ourselves, is the belief that something is inherently wrong with us. In her famous TED Talk "Listening to Shame," Brown describes the difference between guilt and shame: guilt has a focus on behavior while shame has a focus on the self. Brown says, "The guilt within us would say, 'I *made* a mistake'. The shame within us would say, 'I *am* a mistake'."

However, there is an evolutionary reason for the emotion of disgust. Self-judgement is prompted by the need to belong and when we think we're "not enough" in some way, we strive to improve ourselves in order to be accepted. In prehistoric times, if we were not accepted into a tribe, we would not survive. This is why these insecure feelings can sometimes feel like a matter of life or death.

When we recognize that feeling shame has less to do with our worth and more to do with the survival of our species, we expand our perspective and remember that the inner critic is here for a reason. The more we are mindful of the inner critic, the less we identify with it and the quieter it becomes. Also, since this lens of discernment that we use to view ourselves is the same lens we use to view the world, when we soften the inner critic, we subsequently become less judgmental of others.

Calming the Anxiety

Fear is a natural response to stimuli that is perceived as unsafe or threatening. Fear, in and of itself, is not a problem—this emotion has kept humans safe from predators for millennia. The problem is when we overthink our circumstances and fall into a spinning cycle of imagining worst-case scenarios—the "what if …?" nature of the mind quickly goes into overdrive.

With repetitive fearful thoughts, we can become chronically anxious, resulting in seeing *all* circumstances through the lens of fear. Many people turn to food, alcohol, drugs, or work to distract themselves from their ever-present anxiety. Mindfulness can help us break out of this fear cycle. Rather than avoid fear or try to get rid of it, we can simply observe it with mindfulness.

We can also value our fear since it's what keeps us alive—it prompts us to look both ways when crossing the street or call the doctor when we feel pain. Fear is our friend in that it helps us predict and avoid potential threats. Bringing mindfulness to our fearful thoughts provides the clarity to discern whether or not the threat is actually dangerous.

Even if our anxiety never goes away, it's helpful to remember that it can be managed with consistent mindfulness practice. Daily meditation practice can serve as a safe haven for our anxiety to rest.

Cooling the Anger

Anger is a natural human emotion linked to evolution since we needed to fight for resources to survive. Feeling angry during the course of the day is natural, however, with the repetition of angry thoughts, we can develop a "short fuse." Wearing "angry glasses" we can quickly become defensive and have such thoughts as: *What did she mean by that? Is he disrespecting me? No one is going to mess with me!*

Many people enjoy feeling angry because it promotes a false sense of power. But with so much reactivity, we lose clarity on the given situation. Observing the emotion of anger—while not judging ourselves for having it—allows the space for clarity and wisdom to arise.

We can value our anger since it's the appropriate response to an injustice and it motivates us to take action. The key is to find the right amount of anger to stand up for what's right while still seeing the circumstance clearly.

This balanced mindset can be achieved with mindfulness since it shifts the brain activity from the amygdala (the site of fight-or-flight in the brain) to the prefrontal cortex (the site of reasoning). From there, we can communicate and take action against the injustice from a rational state of mind.

Another way to cool our anger is to repeat such phrases as: *This other person is doing the best they can. Their hurtful behavior reveals that they are hurting inside and therefore need compassion.*

Releasing the Sadness

As with all of these feelings, sadness is a natural part of the spectrum of human emotion. There is nothing wrong with feeling sad; it is an appropriate response to the inevitable difficulties in life.

Like dark clouds passing in the sky, it's natural for sadness to come and go in our experience. But when sadness becomes chronic, it is essential to take some time for emotional wellbeing and offer ourselves kindness and compassion.

The gift of sadness is that it arises when it's time to release something that isn't working in our lives. When we cry, we let go of an idea, a belief, or a person that no longer serves us. Knowing that sadness is a signal that we need to let something go, we can welcome it rather than push it away. Bringing mindfulness to our sadness provides the clarity of mind to ask ourselves, *What do I need to let go of?*

After a cathartic cry, we typically feel more relaxed, clear, and open to receive. When we let go of the past, we create the space for something new. Therefore, sadness helps us to move forward in life and is essential for our evolution.

With the tool of mindfulness, we have more control over our emotional experience than we might think. With daily practice, we are no longer at the mercy of these "negative" emotions since we know how to acknowledge, value, and work with them rather than resist them. By tending to these emotions with mindfulness, we can become the architect of our internal experience.

Mixing the Primary Colors of Emotion

Just as a painter combines primary colors to create a full palette, our primary emotions of disgust, fear, anger, and sadness blend to create a vast spectrum of complex emotions, such as jealousy, panic, rage, or melancholy.

Along with the swirling of emotions within ourselves, we also interact with other humans having complicated internal experiences. There are constant misunderstandings since we perceive each other's behavior through our own filters of fear, anger, sadness, or disgust. One person's sadness can trigger another person's fear. One person's disgust can trigger another person's anger. We are continually interacting in a web of emotions and can easily get caught up in the drama. It's a wonder we get along at all.

With mindfulness, we can break out of this web and gain a clear perspective on what's really going on within ourselves and in our relationships. Mindfulness helps us to cultivate a nonreactive and nonjudgmental mindset toward ourselves, others, and our life circumstances.

With our judgments aside, we become more patient and understanding with each other's patterns, perspectives, and intentions that may be different than our own. With less reactivity, we develop deeper connections and have more fulfilling relationships.

Happiness Doesn't Exist without Sadness

We can also value our "negative" emotions in that they serve the purpose of providing contrast. If we never experienced sadness, we would not appreciate joy. If we never experienced frustration, we would not savor contentment. If we never experienced fear, we would not be grateful when we felt safe. A happy life cannot be without darkness—the word happy loses its meaning if it's not balanced by sadness.

Zen Buddhist master, Thich Nhat Hanh, says that suffering is required for us to experience true happiness. Hanh expresses this sentiment and encourages us to value both the good and the bad in our lives in the following passage from his book *No Mud, No Lotus:*

"Without mud, there can be no lotus. You can't grow lotus flowers on marble. It is possible to get stuck in the 'mud' of life. We must remember that suffering is a kind of mud that we need in order to generate joy and happiness. Without suffering, there's no happiness. So, we shouldn't discriminate against the mud."

So, rather than resisting our difficult circumstances or painful emotions, we can welcome them, offer them appreciation, and see them as opportunities for growth. If our anger, anxiety, and depression are the "mud" in life, our mindfulness practice can be the "fertilizer" that transforms our consciousness into the strength and wisdom of the "lotus flower."

Valuing the Full Spectrum of our Emotions is Valuing Life Itself

Our fluctuating emotions can feel like a roller coaster, but mindfulness can be the seatbelt, allowing us to feel safe and grounded as we experience the highest of highs and lowest of lows. With the help of mindfulness, we can view all of life's challenges as valuable since they serve as opportunities to practice and increase our awareness. If we resist, avoid, or distract ourselves from our heavy emotions, we miss powerful opportunities for awakening.

It's important to remember that a rich, satisfying, and enjoyable life is not perfect all the time. As human beings, we experience a wide range of complicated emotions. When things go well, we celebrate. When things go poorly, we feel pain, but we also learn and grow. Appreciating the entire spectrum of emotions, not just the "positive" ones, makes us complete human beings since we are not shutting down or pushing away any part of ourselves.

As long as we are alive, we will experience these challenging emotions. But, when we value *all* of our feelings, we value life itself and we don't take our precious lives for granted. By valuing both the joy and the pain, we honor the full spectrum of our emotions, have a richer life experience, and appreciate the incredible gift it is to be alive as a human being.

The Value Practice Meditation

> Listen to the meditation online at:
> **www.meditationforbreastcancer.com**

Let's begin by gently closing your eyes or lowering your gaze. Feeling your feet on the floor. Lifting up your spine and relaxing your shoulders, arms and back. Allowing your hands to rest wherever they are comfortable.

Taking a few deep breaths in and out through the nose. Allowing the body to soften. Allowing the mind to settle. Bringing your attention to your chest. Noticing how your chest rises on the inhale and falls on the exhale. Sustaining your attention on the breath flowing in and out of the chest. Breath flows in, the chest rises, breath flows out, the chest falls. Establishing your anchor, feeling the sensations of the breath at the chest area.

I invite you to think about a challenging circumstance you're facing in your life right now. What is the emotion that comes up due to this circumstance? Is it fear, anger, or sadness? Choose one emotion for this exercise.

Take a deep breath in and give this emotion your full attention. Say to yourself, *I am not alone in feeling this way. This is a natural human emotion. Others would feel the same in this circumstance.*

Take in another deep breath and feel the connection with every other person who has also felt this emotion. Take a moment to value this emotion. Even though it's painful, it has brought you to this beautiful experience of connection with every other human being on this planet. Take another deep breath and feel that connection deeply.

We can also value this emotion because it has something to teach us. Anxiety may be revealing that you need to feel safe. Anger reveals your ethics, your boundaries, and what you stand for. Sadness reveals your deep desires in life, or that it's time to let something go. I invite you to ask your emotion, *Why are you here? What do you have to teach me?*

We can also value this emotion because it provides contrast. Without anger, we cannot know contentment. Without sadness, we cannot know happiness. Without anxiety, we cannot know ease. Take a moment to value the full spectrum of our emotions, both the light and the shadow, for we cannot have one without the other.

When we welcome *all* of our emotions, rather than judge ourselves for the negative ones, we honor the full human experience and we don't take our precious lives for granted.

Taking in another deep breath and bring both hands to your heart and befriend your emotion. Say to your emotion, "Thank you for being here. Thank you for bringing me to my meditation cushion today, and guiding me deeper into my practice and deeper into my heart. Thank you, for enriching my life and connecting me with others. Thank you for showing me the full spectrum of what it is to be human and for being instrumental in my spiritual growth. I give thanks for every day that I have the opportunity to feel this emotion. You are a reminder that I am alive as a human being on this beautiful planet, and I am grateful for the precious gift of life."

Taking one another deep breath, allowing gratitude to fill your body and radiate outward. Gently bring your focus back to your anchor, back the sensation of your breath at you chest area. On the inhale the chest rises, on the exhale the chest falls.

As we begin to close the meditation, feel your legs on the cushion or chair beneath you. Gently wiggle your fingers and toes. Whenever you're ready, end the meditation and gently open your eyes.

Part 4
"E" *is for* Embrace

Chapter 10
All We Need Is Love

"The point is not to try to throw ourselves away and become something better. It's about befriending who we are already."
Pema Chödrön, Buddhist nun

Getting Cancer Isn't Cheap

Having cancer not only affected my physical body; it affected every aspect of my life—my relationships, my career, and my finances.

Since I'd lost my job, I was able to collect unemployment, however, I lost my health insurance. To make sure I didn't have a lapse in coverage, I immediately signed up for Cobra. A letter about my new Cobra policy had been sitting on my kitchen counter for a few days. Although I was still adjusting to having cancer, I knew I'd have to face how much money this year of treatment would cost.

I opened the letter and read the premium amount. My eyes widened, *Seven hundred dollars per month?* I had a tough time wrapping my head around that amount since I typically paid around two hundred dollars a month for health insurance.

I picked up a calculator and quickly did the math to figure out how much this would cost for the year. *Wow, I'll need $8,400 this year to pay for this plan! I don't have a job. How am I going to afford this?*

My savings account balance was roughly seven thousand dollars, but this was my vacation fund. I had been putting money aside for the last three years to walk the Camino in Spain. *I guess I'll kiss that dream good-bye*, I thought. *Instead of a trip to Spain, I'll be spending my savings on chemo and surgeries. Great. That's just great.*

My phone buzzed. It was a text from my friend Alyssa saying she would be over in five minutes. Alyssa and I had completed a meditation teacher training earlier that year, and we'd become very close.

The doorbell rang, and I opened the door. "Hi, Sharon!" Alyssa said.

"Hey sister," I said, offering her a hug. "Come on in. How are you?"

"I'm doing great," she said, offering me a bottle of wine and a slice of tiramisu from my favorite bakery. "The real question is, how are *you*?"

"I'm doing alright, hanging in there. Thank you for this," I said, receiving her gifts. "Make yourself at home," gesturing to the sofa.

I retrieved two wine glasses from the kitchen, poured the wine, and sat down next to my friend. I handed her a glass and said, "Cheers."

"Aw, cheers to you, my dear!" she said, and we clinked glasses. "So, you had your second chemo last week, right? How are you feeling?"

"I'm doing okay," I said, and then I began to cry.

"What's wrong, Sharon?" she asked. "What's going on?"

"I didn't want to say anything. But I just looked at my health insurance bill and it's outrageous," I said. "I shouldn't bring it up, but I'll say this, 'Cancer ain't cheap'."

"Oh, honey. That's terrible," she said, putting her wine glass on the coffee table. "I'm so sorry."

"Yeah, well, the hardest part is that I'd been saving money to take this trip to Spain," I said. "Have you heard of the Camino?"

"Yes, I walked the Camino a few years ago. It's amazing!" she said. "Oh, you *have* to go!"

Her comment turned my disappointment into resentment. I took another sip of wine and started to vent.

"I just can't believe it. I already have to deal with a life-threatening disease, putting poison into my body, losing my hair, and feeling like I'm a 90-year-old woman. Not to mention losing my breast in a couple of months, and my fertility," I said through my tears. "But on top of *all* of that, I am going to go broke, too?"

"I'm so sorry, honey," she said. "I'm so sorry."

"Yeah, well, I know there's nothing I can do about it. I just needed to vent," I said. "Obviously, my health is more important than taking a vacation. I just want my life back, you know?"

"Yeah, I hear you, love," she said. "And you will, you will get your life back. But for now, let's just focus on getting you healthy. That's what is most important now."

"Yeah, you're right," I said. "I'll just take one step at a time and focus on my healing for now. Spain will be … another time. Thank you so much for listening."

What to Say When a Loved One is Diagnosed with Cancer

Although Alyssa was a caring listener and held space for me as I vented, one of the biggest challenges I had while going through treatment was navigating the constant barrage of people's opinions about cancer. From what foods to eat to whether or not to do chemotherapy, the unsolicited advice never stopped.

Even when offered with the best intentions, this advice was harmful in that it made me question the treatments that were already taking place. I had already decided on the treatments of chemo, surgery, and radiation and since I had a life-threatening illness, I held on to this decision as if it was my lifeline, therefore, any doubt about its efficacy caused my fear of death to skyrocket.

When talking to a friend going through cancer treatment, it's important to remember how fragile their psyches are. They might be saying to themselves, "If I make the wrong choice regarding my treatment, I will die." They are desperately holding on to hope, and their belief in their chosen medical team and treatment must be rock-solid to keep their mental health intact. The mind is incredibly powerful, so whatever one's belief regarding what is best for them must be respected.

As we've seen with placebo experiments, your friend's belief in their chosen treatment may be the very thing that saves them. Therefore, when it's a life-or-death situation, it's crucial to not poke holes of doubt in your friend's belief by suggesting treatments that are counter to what they've already decided.

The truth is, once I had decided on my treatment plan, all I needed from people around me was to respect my decision and support me. But since I was in the spiritual community, I had many friends urge me to take the all-natural route and even judge me for opting for Western medicine. The pain of being judged on top of dealing with the stress of my illness was agonizing. After each piece of unwanted advice, I would often say to my friend, "I don't need any more information; I just need your support."

Another conversation that was challenging was when people tried to figure out the cause of my cancer. Being in the spiritual community, many friends implied that I developed cancer due to a metaphysical reason, such as my chakras were not balanced, my heart was blocked because I was single, or because I wasn't living my purpose.

These theories are not only inaccurate, but they are also hurtful. They fall into the category of victim-blaming in that they imply that people who are diagnosed with cancer *deserved* it somehow, or that they did something to *cause* it. These theories aren't proven to be true, they don't help, and they only make the patient who already feels terrible to feel even worse.

It seemed that people were obsessed with figuring out the cause of my cancer because they were afraid of getting cancer themselves. They thought if they could identify why it happened to me (someone in their 40s who led a healthy lifestyle) they could avoid it happening in their own lives. But the truth is, I had no idea why cancer developed in my body—no one knew for sure. So rather than focusing on the cause, it was more helpful when friends simply offered compassion and support.

The *most* challenging discussion, however, was when people came up to me and listed off all of the people they knew who had died from breast cancer. On a daily basis, people would say to me, "Hey Sharon, I heard you have breast cancer. That's too bad. My mom died of breast cancer." Or, "My aunt died of breast cancer."

I would typically respond with, "I'm sorry to hear that." And then quickly change the subject. But in my head, I was thinking, *Thanks for providing more evidence that death is a possibility for me. Thanks for adding more fuel to my fear of death!*

Again, I know that people's intentions were good, and they were sharing their experiences with cancer because they wanted to connect with me, but because the fear of death was at the forefront of my mind, it was painful to hear. For many, receiving a cancer diagnosis is equated with a death sentence. So the best way to care for them emotionally is to avoid the topic of death, ask them how they would like to be supported, and only share stories about people who have survived cancer and are now thriving—fuel the hope, not the fear.

Learning to Trust Myself

Even with my requests for the contrary, the morbid stories and unsolicited advice continued to pour in. Realizing that this avalanche was not going to stop, I had to, once again, drop into surrender. Rather than resist, I accepted the notion that it was natural human behavior to want to fix a problem, sound knowledgeable, and pinpoint the cause.

From this surrendered place, I began to trust myself. I began to tune out other people's opinions like white noise and listen deep within. When it was time to make a decision about my health, along with discussing options with my doctors, I turned inward and asked my inner guidance. I trusted that these intuitive answers were the best courses of treatment for me and my body.

Eventually, it no longer bothered me when people shared their traumatic stories about cancer, because I knew those where *their* stories, not mine. By turning inward, I strengthened my resolve to move through this journey with strength and positivity. I was writing *my* story, and even if death would be the outcome of this cancer journey, my story would still be one of hope, gratitude, and love.

Halfway through the Marathon

It was July 30, and I had just completed my third infusion. This treatment marked the midway point for my six tough chemo sessions.

For the first three, I was pumped up. I was proud of my organized schedule, and I was going deeper into meditation with each round. Now, I was over the thrill of "taking on" cancer, but I couldn't yet see the light at the end of the tunnel. It had been exactly three months since I'd been diagnosed. I had two more months and three more sessions to go, and I was over it.

A few days before chemo session number four, a rush of anxiety arose. Every infusion felt like bombs were dropped into my bloodstream. I had felt so good during my third week, and I didn't want to go back into the fire.

By then, I knew what to expect regarding the side effects. With my mindfulness practice, I knew I could handle whatever came up physically or emotionally. I had overcome this first hurdle of managing the side effects, and now it was time to learn the next lesson—*perseverance*.

As a meditator, I acknowledged that this anxious impatience was an opportunity to dig deeper and cultivate patience. I surrendered to the fact that I had three more sessions of chemo to go and attempted to embody grace with quiet perseverance.

When I felt impatient and frustrated, I did a mini-practice of asking myself, *How do I feel right now, at this moment?*

Usually, the answer was, *I feel okay*. This simple question was helpful to shift my mind from the future to the present moment, and experience some ease.

Where Else Can You Touch Me?

During these five months of chemotherapy, my body physically got weaker and weaker, and it took a considerable toll on my skin, nails, and hair. But I kept up my enthusiasm about Will and thoroughly enjoyed going on dates with this kind and handsome man.

On one of our dates in Laguna Beach, we had dinner at a gorgeous restaurant on the beach and then headed back to our hotel. The hotel room had two beds, and the moment we opened the door Will began to passionately kiss me and we fell onto bed number one. After a few minutes, I looked down at the bed and saw that it was covered with my hair. I was mortified and hoped that he didn't notice.

"Hey," I said. "Let's hop onto the other bed."

He shrugged his shoulders and said, "Okay, sure!"

We jumped onto the second bed and continued our make-out session. Once again, my hair was shedding all over the place. It was too obvious, so I had to say something.

"So, let's play a game," I said. "My hair is falling out really easily, so rather than massage the back of my head when you kiss me, can you put your hand somewhere else? The game is called 'Where else can you touch me?'"

He chuckled and said, "That works for me!"

The next morning, I went to the bathroom and noticed my hair in the mirror. Overnight, my hair had turned into the texture of straw, and I had six little dreadlocks spiraling out of my scalp.

"Damn it," I whispered. I was hoping to keep my hair long, but looking at my reflection, I knew I would have to cut it short.

"Good morning," said Will as he rolled over in bed and looked up at me standing in the bathroom.

"Hey," I said, wistfully. "My hair also had a party last night. It looks like I'll have to cut it."

"That's okay," he said. "You'll look cute with short hair."

I smiled and got back into bed and into his arms.

"So, when is your surgery?" he asked.

"It's in two months," I said. "I'm having the mastectomy and then reconstruction on the same day. They are taking fat from my stomach to create my breast instead of inserting an implant. Supposedly it will feel more natural that way."

"Well, I'll be the judge of that," he said with a smile. "Are you nervous about it?"

"Yeah, of course," I said. "But I have a good plastic surgeon, so I hope it will look okay."

I was not only nervous about the surgery itself but also how it would affect my relationship with Will. Sure, I would have a reconstructed breast, but I didn't know how much sensation the new breast would have or how the scars or tattoo would turn out. I also didn't know if the surgeon would be able to match the new breast with the original in size and shape.

Basically, I had no idea if I would still be attractive to Will (or *any* man) after the procedure, and this uncertainty was crushing.

"I'm sure you'll be fine, and I'm sure you'll look beautiful," he said, as if reading my mind. "Since you'll be making so many appointments with all of these doctors, will you make appointments with me, too?"

"Yeah, that sounds good," I said, appreciating his kindness. "So ... do you want to be Dr. Feel-Good or Dr. Love?"

"Dr. Love. Definitely, Dr. Love," he said. "And you tell those breast surgeons that Dr. Love will be checking up on their work."

Chapter 11

Treat Yourself Like Someone You Love

"You yourself, as much as anybody in the entire universe, deserve your love and affection."
Sharon Salzberg, meditation teacher

Chemo Treats Cancer, Compassion Treats Suffering

In my mind, I had successfully separated the two concepts of pain and suffering. The pain was the cancer in my body, and the suffering was my *reaction* to the cancer. I had to let go of worrying about treating the cancer (that was my doctor's job) and instead, I put all of my energy into soothing my suffering with mindfulness. Among the various practices, I discovered that self-compassion was the most effective remedy. Just as chemotherapy was the medicine to treat my cancer, compassion was the medicine to treat my suffering.

During the five months of chemotherapy, I attended a weekly mindfulness class. My teacher, Heather, explained how compassion alleviates suffering with the following anecdote:

"Let's say a child falls down, skins her knee, and starts to cry. When her mother comes to hold her, the child stops crying. Although the wound on the knee and the physical pain are still there, the child's suffering is relieved by her mother's compassion. The same thing happens with self-compassion—when we offer ourselves compassion, we can soothe our own suffering, even if the pain is still present."

I put this theory that self-compassion would alleviate my suffering to the test. I treated my body as if it were an infant—keeping it out of the sun, making sure it was hydrated, and protecting it from crowds and loud noises, as well as prioritizing relaxation. It was kind of sweet. I had never given my physical body that much caring attention before. I enjoyed the opportunity to nurture myself.

I had self-care regimens, daily meditations, and weekly medications, but the most important aspect of my wellbeing was quieting the inner critic and offering love and compassion toward my thoughts and emotions. It was during these five months of chemotherapy that I learned how to love myself.

Self-compassion practices also apply to physical pain. I spoke to Heather about the side effects of chemo and that I was often scared by the pain. She offered this advice:

"If you're in fear, you're abandoning the body," said Heather. "Instead, stay with the pain. Give it the love and care it's crying out for with your self-compassion practice. Don't abandon the body."

Following my teacher's instructions, I chose to observe the pain with curiosity when a side effect arose, rather than go into fear. I would also add compassion by placing my hand on the location of the pain and say, "I hear you. I love you. How can I help? What do you need?"

Offering this heartfelt compassion dissolved any fears in that moment, and sometimes it alleviated the pain itself. Other times I took a pain reliever along with doing this self-compassion practice. Either way, I was addressing both the physical pain and the emotional suffering.

As an ongoing act of self-compassion, I asked myself this question throughout the day, *What is the most self-loving choice I can make right now?*

Typically, the answer was to stop whatever I was doing, take some deep breaths, put on some beautiful music, and take a nap. Giving myself permission to slow down and rest my body was a necessary part of my self-compassion and self-care practices.

We Can Hold Ourselves

Two days after my fourth chemo session, my short hair continued to spin into dreadlocks. In a fit of frustration, I picked up a comb and a pair of scissors to cut out the mini dreads. Chunks of hair were still falling out of my scalp, and with every strand that fell, I got even more upset. *Why aren't the cold caps working?*

While looking in a mirror cutting the dreadlocks, I lost focus and cut my left hand. Blood started pouring out everywhere. I recalled a conversation I'd had with a nurse who told me that my blood-platelet counts were low, so if I cut myself, there was the potential to bleed out. *I could bleed out! No!*

In a panic, I fell to my knees. I held my hands above my head and applied pressure to the wound. I took a few deep breaths, looked at my bleeding hand and began the self-compassion practice. I said to myself, as if speaking sweetly to an injured child, *This is a hard moment, Sharon. But I've got you. I love you. I'll take care of you. You're going to be okay.*

Even though my hand was still throbbing in pain, the kind words brought some relief to my nervous system. I was able to catch my breath and began to think more clearly. Just like the mother who held her child that fell and skinned her knee—*I was able to hold myself.*

Once my mind calmed down, I remembered that I'd gotten blood work done the day before, so I picked up the phone and called my doctor. In a two-minute phone call, my doctor reported that my blood-platelet counts were back to normal. She reassured me that I had nothing to worry about. *What a relief!*

I bandaged up my hand and reflected on that emotional journey. Within five minutes, my mindfulness practice helped me shift from a state of panic to a balanced mindset, which allowed me to make that phone call to my doctor. It was empowering to know that even though I didn't have control over my circumstance, my mindfulness practice offered some control over my emotions.

The Difference between Self-Care and Self-Love

Because of my consistent self-compassion practice, I realized that self-love was not about getting massages or taking bubble baths—that was self-care. Self-love was lovingly listening to what my mind and body were expressing and tending to those messages with caring, compassionate awareness. Rather than judging my thoughts or emotions, I observed them and met them all with kindness.

In his book *No Mud, No Lotus*, Buddhist monk Thich Nhat Hanh says that when we observe our emotions and meet them with compassion, our loving awareness transforms our negative emotions into *itself*, i.e., more loving awareness is created. The scientist in me understood the concept that energy was always moving and changing. So since our emotions are composed of energy, I was on board with this idea that emotions can morph into something new.

As I sat in meditation, I took a few deep breaths and visualized my awareness as a spotlight of love shining onto the emotion of fear. After a few minutes, I experienced the fear transforming and dissolving, and becoming engulfed by the spotlight of love. By the end of my meditation, the emotion of fear was gone, and I felt a strong sensation of loving energy in my chest.

I recognized that the transformation of my fear did not occur when I tried to fix the given problem or push the emotion away. The transformation happened when I observed and cared for the emotion directly.

Every time I meditated, I was transforming my suffering into love. The more I observed my emotions with loving eyes, the more my loving awareness expanded. With my self-compassion practice, I had befriended my inner experience and I learned what self-love really is—the consistent offering of compassion to one's own thoughts and emotions.

The Mindful Gardener

Another way I relaxed during these five months of chemotherapy was working in my garden. Since I brought my full attention to the colors of the vegetables and the sensations of the cool soil on my hands, gardening had become another informal mindfulness practice that brought me into the ease of the present moment.

While tending to my garden, I created an analogy between the garden and my body. If a particular plant was growing too fast and overtaking the rest of the plants, I wouldn't get upset. As a mindful gardener, I would tend to the health of the garden as a whole. Perhaps I'd spray a chemical onto the troublesome plant (chemotherapy) and pull it out of the garden (surgery). I would certainly pay loving attention to the other plants (the rest of my body) and make sure the soil of the garden (my mental and emotional wellbeing) was optimally nourished.

The truth is, our bodies are not separate from nature. Since our physical form consists of the same organic material as a garden—carbon, hydrogen, oxygen, nitrogen, etc.—our bodies are subject to the same laws of nature where glitches occur frequently. It's the human mind that catastrophizes and thinks that these natural events are abnormal in some way. But our bodies are part of the earth, which is organic matter continually shifting out of balance and then course-correcting back into equilibrium. We see this happening in nature all the time, and our bodies are just the same.

The Strength of a Mountain

During chemotherapy, my body aged at a faster rate than usual. This rapid deterioration of my physical appearance was incredibly hard on my self-esteem. I gained weight and lost strength in my muscles. My skin became sallow, and my eyes lost their twinkle.

The hardest part was the change in my hair, which was falling out in patches all around my head. I didn't mind the hair loss from the rest of my body (that was convenient, actually), but losing hair from my head was devastating. My long and wavy hair was a big part of my identity as a feminine woman. Having short and thin hair, I no longer recognized myself when I looked in the mirror.

Taking showers was particularly tough because my hair would fall out in my hands in clumps. Looking at my hair covering the shower floor, I'd drop my head and cry as the water washed over me. The shower was the one place I didn't have to keep it all together and pretend that I was okay. Since no one could hear me in the shower, I often unleashed the floodgates and cried.

The gradual process of losing my hair was parallel to the unfolding realization that I didn't have control in life. This realization didn't happen overnight. It was not until I had done everything in my power not to lose my hair—including buying special brushes, cutting my hair short, and wearing those painful ice packs during treatments—and *still* lost the majority of my hair, that I had no other choice but to surrender control completely.

By the time I finished my fifth chemotherapy treatment, I had lost about seventy percent of my hair, and I was too emotionally exhausted to resist it any longer. *What will be, will be.*

That night, I called my friend Sabrina, a dear friend and breast cancer survivor, and asked her how she coped with the grief of hair loss during treatment.

"Oh, I remember losing a lot of hair during showers. Yeah, that was awful," Sabrina said. "But that's when I dug deep for my strength. In the shower, I stood up tall with dignity. Even if I'd lost all of my hair, which I did, I was still *me* on the inside, and cancer could never take that away."

After the call, I stepped into the shower and remembered Sabrina's inspiring words. Instead of breaking down into tears, I took a deep breath, lifted my chest, and extended my arms down at my sides. I stood in the powerful yoga pose *Tadasana* and embodied the strength of a mountain as the warm water washed over me.

With my head held high, I was letting go of the need for my hair and body to look a certain way. With each deep breath, I was committed to loving myself no matter what I looked like physically. In that power pose, I remembered that no matter how many locks of hair fell out of my head, my Spirit would always be powerful, beautiful, whole and complete.

Standing powerfully in the shower, I thought to myself, *I am not my hair; I am my Spirit. With every hair that falls out, my Spirit shines brighter.*

Reconciling with Death

A week before my sixth and final chemo session, my mind and body were completely exhausted. Even though it had been five months since diagnosis, the fear of death was still a reoccurring emotion.

On one of my daily walks, I noticed a group of plants clumped together around the base of an oak tree. In my field of vision, I saw the entire circle of life—young plants, mature plants, and dead plants transitioning back into the earth. I realized the degradation of organic debris was creating space for seedlings to emerge—*if there was no death, there would be no new life*.

As I stood there, looking at this vision of natural perfection while chemo was swirling in my bloodstream, I realized the same process was happening in my body. Some cells were dying, some cells were clearing out of my system, and some cells were growing anew.

I closed my eyes and imagined this churning cycle within—*death and rebirth, death and rebirth*. I began to understand that all living things experienced birth, growth, and death. Everything was changing at all times—everything was impermanent.

The understanding of this natural cycle reduced my fear of death. Since death was a natural part of this cycle, it was no longer something to fear. I could either resist this natural cycle occurring within my body or surrender to the process.

I had initially been afraid of chemotherapy, and I prayed for the medicine to harm only cancer cells and not the rest of my body. But after looking at the plants around the oak tree, I realized that death was necessary for new growth to occur. And even if the medicine harmed my healthy cells, these cells would exit my body and create space for new cells to emerge.

The Last Chemo

September 12, 2018, marked my sixth and final chemo treatment that had challenging side effects. Today was the last stop of the hard-chemo train.

On my way to my infusion chair, I saw Linda, who was also receiving her final treatment that day. I remembered the first time I met her. It was the first day of chemotherapy for both of us and she had thick, dark hair to her shoulders. Now, we both had the equivalent of peach fuzz on our heads. Linda wore a colorful scarf around her neck, and she was just as beautiful as ever. It felt like we had endured a "life course" together and today was our graduation day.

Mom and Sabrina offer me kisses during my final chemo session.

"Hi, Linda!" I said exuberantly. "We made it! How are you feeling?"

"Hi, Sharon!" she said. "Yes, isn't this exciting? I feel great! It's our last one!"

"Thank you for going on this journey with me," I said. "It was comforting to see your face every time and know that we were going through this together."

Linda gave me a proud smile, and then we both took our seats for our final round. Mom put the cold cap on my head and I put on my headphones to listen to meditations and drop into a surrendered slumber. Sabrina arrived that afternoon to help Mom with the cold caps and keep me company. When the last drop of chemo left the bag, the machine beeped, and I threw my hands into the air and squealed, "YESSSS!! I made it! I'm done!"

Although light-headed and nauseous, I felt victorious. I thanked and hugged my nurses, Ruby and Kelly, who were consistently calm and caring throughout my course of treatment. I walked out of the infusion room like a rock star, waving good-bye to everyone. "Congratulations, Sharon!" said Ruby, with a big smile.

Linda also finished at the same time, and the moment we exited the building we jumped into the air with exhilaration. "We did it! We did it!" we exclaimed, and then gave each other a big hug. I looked at her in the eyes and said, "Well done, sister. All the very best to you."

It was time to celebrate! Mom, Sabrina, and I went to dinner, and we ordered a round of margaritas. I usually didn't drink after chemotherapy, but since this was my final round, I made an exception. Sabrina lifted her cocktail and said, "To Sharon!"

"I'm so proud of you, honey," Sabrina continued. "Finishing chemo is such an accomplishment. You handled it with so much grace. Here's to you!"

Sabrina proved to be an incredible source of support. She always knew what would happen next on the journey, and it meant everything to know that I could call her and ask her anything.

Mom lifted her drink, looked at me, and paused. Her proud expression brought a tear to my eyes. She had been there for every appointment and every treatment. She was my rock and my angel.

"To my beautiful daughter," Mom said. "I'm so proud of you. You've brought so much love and light to my life and so many around you. May you have a long, healthy, and beautiful life. You deserve it."

"Aww, thank you, Mom," I said, with tears welling up in my eyes. And then we all took a drink. "That was so sweet, thank you."

We thoroughly enjoyed our dinner and celebrated the triumph of the occasion. I came home to find a dozen red roses on my doorstep. I read the card, "Congratulations! You made it! Love, Will." The roses brought a smile to my face. I sent Will a text thanking him, then laid down on my bed. Relishing in the sense of accomplishment, I fell into a deep, blissful sleep.

An Unexpected Outcome: Zero Side Effects

A couple of days later, I braced myself for the last round of side effects. My oncologist said the side effects would be cumulative, meaning that my final round would be the hardest. But something remarkable happened—I didn't have *any* side effects.

I attributed this unexpected outcome to my daily mindfulness practice. I believe that side effects are the result of the body retaliating against the chemo. But since I had reassured my cells that these chemicals were not invaders, but instead here to help, my body was relaxed while receiving chemo and welcomed the medicine. My practice caused my mind to be less reactive, which caused the cells of my body to be less resistant to the medicine, resulting in fewer side effects.

My oncologist also said the results of my weekly blood tests often looked like someone not going through chemotherapy. Again, another testament to my mindfulness practice calming my nervous system so effectively that it was having a positive influence on my physical health.

My blood test results, and not having side effects after my final chemo session, were evidence of the mind-body connection. With daily mindfulness practices, I cultivated safety and ease in my body rather than resistance. Over the course of my six rounds of chemo, I'd noticed that when I was anxious, the side effects were worse compared to when my mind was calm. But to have *zero* side effects when I was supposed to have the most was extraordinary and a real testament to the power of mindfulness!

Compassionate Body Scan Meditation

Practice after Chemotherapy

Listen to the meditation online at:
www.meditationforbreastcancer.com

For this meditation, many people lie down on the floor, either completely flat or with the lower legs up on a chair. But you're welcome to sit on a cushion or a chair, if you prefer. Go ahead and place your body into the position that is most comfortable for you at this time.

Let's start by first getting in touch with your entire body. How does your whole body feel right now? See if you can feel the weight of your body either on the floor or on the cushion or chair. Notice any body sensations; any heaviness, lightness, tingling, achiness? Feeling your entire body, just as it is, in this moment.

During this compassionate body scan meditation, we will move our awareness from the crown of the head through the body and down to the toes. Given your recent treatments, we will stop and offer compassion for the parts of your body that are experiencing tension or painful side-effects. We will also offer gratitude to your organs that are working so hard to detoxify your body. By offering compassion, your body will begin to feel safe and relaxed, allowing the natural healing intelligence of the body to proceed.

Let's start with the crown of the head. Notice what sensations are there. See if you can tune into the point just above your head. Do you feel any tingling? If you don't feel anything, that's okay too.

Now become aware of your facial muscles. The muscles in our face work very hard when we express our emotions. To release tension in your facial muscles, imagine caressing your face with your awareness, relaxing the muscles starting with the forehead, relaxing between the eyebrows, the temples, the cheeks, the jaw, relaxing the muscles of the jaw, and allow your mouth to slightly fall open.

Now notice any sensations on the tongue. Is there tingling? Soreness? Perhaps a metallic sensation? Once you've labeled the sensation, rather than judge it or react to it, simply allow it to be there. Perhaps with some curiosity, notice how this sensation might shift.

Now become aware of how your neck feels. Any tension or tightness? Your neck holds up our heavy head and can hold a lot of tension. So, relax the neck muscles and soothe and comfort any points of pain you may be experiencing.

Dropping down into your shoulders and upper back. A lot of emotional tension, fear, and stress is held in this area. What sensations do you feel here? Heat? Cold? Tightness? Achiness? With your loving awareness, soothing any feelings of discomfort you may have. Imagine getting a little massage around the shoulders and upper back. Soothing your muscles with your awareness.

Now bring your awareness to your upper arms. Kindly caressing the upper arms down toward the elbows and noticing any sensations that are there. Allowing the sensations to be just as they are. Continuing to move your loving awareness down the arms to your wrists, hands, and fingers, pausing to soothe and offer compassion to any tension that might be there. Take a moment to offer gratitude for all that our hands do for us. Let yourself be amazed at how intricate your hands are and how much they enrich your life.

Now bring your attention to the chest area, the home of your heart. This is where emotions are often felt very intensely. Noticing any physical sensations in the chest area. Is there a buzzing? A tingling? Do you feel a tightness? A heaviness? Now notice your heart beating. Is it beating quickly or slowly? Remember that one sensation is not better than the other, we are simply noticing what's there, and relaxing around the sensations. Offer comfort toward yourself for any physical or emotional pain you might be feeling in your chest.

Bring one hand to your heart, and take a moment to feel your heartbeat. Take a deep breath and say "thank you" to your loving heart. For your entire life, your heart has kept a consistent beat, it has kept you alive and strong. It is also the source of your love and compassion. Your beautiful heart is a furnace of love. Offer gratitude for your enduring, life-affirming heart. Say "thank you" for keeping a steady beat during this tender time in your life. Release your hand to the side.

Now bring your attention to your stomach area. Noticing any physical sensations in the abdomen, any tension, discomfort, or movement. A lot of difficult emotions get stored here, including fear. Oftentimes when we feel anxious, it's as if our stomach is in knots. Remember, we are not trying to change any sensation, we are just noticing them, letting them be, and offering them some compassion.

Now let's shift our attention to the liver, the primary detoxing organ of the body. Place one hand on your liver, which is located in the upper right side of the abdomen. Offering gratitude through the palm of your hand, say "thank you" to your liver, thank you for working so hard to detox the chemotherapy and other medicines from the body.

As you're offering thanks and appreciation, visualize the liver cleansing and extracting any medicine from the blood and sending it down the intestinal tract to exit the body.

The intestines are often a place we experience side-effects from chemotherapy. Slowly and gently massage your abdomen in a clockwise direction, mirroring the direction of the intestines. As you circle your hand around the navel, if you feel any painful sensation, pause and offer love and compassion to that area. If you're experiencing constipation as a side-effect, as you're circling you can occasionally stop and press a little firmer with a gentle shaking action to break up any stagnation.

You can also visualize the medicine exiting the body through the colon while taking deep breaths and elongating the exhale. As you're visualizing the chemotherapy leaving the body, you can say to it, "Thank you for clearing out malignant cells from my body, but your job is done here, and you can leave now." Visualizing the lining of the intestines clean, shiny, and rejuvenated back to health.

It can be hard to be in this physical body that experiences so many different painful sensations, so let us be kind to ourselves in this moment and offer our body the soothing balm of compassion.

Next let's offer compassion and appreciation to our kidneys, which detox our bodies through the urinary tract. First focusing your attention on your breath at your abdomen. Feel the sensation of the rise and fall of the belly as you breathe in and out. Place the palms of both hands onto your kidneys, located on your lower back on either side of your spinal column. Placing gentle pressure and taking a few deep breaths, imagine that love and compassion are streaming out of your palms to your kidneys.

Kidneys serve as our storehouse of vitality, steadiness, wisdom, and the power within. Steady your attention onto your kidneys and notice whatever sensations arise. Offer gratitude for your kidneys. Say "thank you" for working so hard to detox the healing medicine from the body. Visualize the medicine traveling from the kidneys, through the urinary tract, and out of the body. Visualize your kidneys thoroughly cleaned and rejuvenated back to health. Release your hands to the sides.

Dropping your attention to your buttocks, feel the weight of your glutes on your cushion, the chair or the floor. Noticing what sensations are there. Is there any tightness or achiness? Soothing and relaxing this part of the body.

Now bring your focus to your upper legs. What do you feel in this part of the body? See if you can relax the thigh muscles. Moving your awareness down the legs past the knees to your calves and shins. Feeling any sensation in these muscles, and softening around any tension. Dropping down to your ankles and feet, and take a moment to notice any tension and relax the muscles in the arches, the soles of the feet, and the toes. Offering yourself a cozy foot massage with your awareness. Take in a deep breath and say "thank you" to both of your feet for allowing you to walk, run, and dance through this beautiful life.

Lastly, bring your attention to the location where the IV was placed from your last infusion. Gently place one hand onto this area and imagine radiant love, healing, and compassion streaming out from the palm of your hand. Open your heart, take a few deep breaths, and offer nurturing compassion from your heart to this wound. Just as a mother might caress and offer loving compassion to a child who is feeling discomfort, take the same comforting and loving attitude with your awareness.

Now widen your focus so that you're aware of the golden life-force energy flowing throughout your entire body. Feeling your own radiant love washing and cleansing your body, starting at the feet, the golden light moves up through the legs, filling the abdomen, chest, and neck, all the way to the top of your head. Feeling the vibrant energy of life flowing through you. Resting in the knowing of your body's resilience and deep appreciation for the body's incredible healing intelligence.

Chapter 12

The Embrace Practice— Embrace the Emotion

"A moment of self-compassion can change your entire day. A string of such moments can change the course of your life."
Christopher Germer, clinical psychologist

What Is Self-compassion, and Why Is It Important?

The first "E" in the LOVEE Method stands for Embrace. We have arrived at the sweet part of the practice, the time when we open our hearts to our own suffering and offer love, care, and compassion to our own emotions.

We can learn about the meaning of compassion by breaking the word down. In Latin, the prefix com- means "with," and -passion means "suffering." Therefore, the translation of the word compassion is "to suffer *with*."[1] To be compassionate means that we care about someone's suffering and we have a desire to alleviate it.

Self-compassion is the urge to help ourselves when *we* are the ones suffering. It's turning our love and care toward ourselves in times of pain.

Self-compassion practices are particularly useful to quiet the inner critic. When someone we care about feels anxious, sad, or angry, most of the time we don't judge them—we care for them and ask how we can help. But often, when we experience these same emotions, the inner critic offers judgment and our self-esteem plummets. Self-compassion involves the process of befriending our feelings rather than judging them, and offering the same level of kindness toward ourselves that we would give to someone we love.

Mindfulness works alongside self-compassion because it creates the pause that offers the opportunity for us to be gentle and kind with ourselves when challenging emotions arise. During the Label and Observe practices, we create the "mindful gap," which is the space between the observing mind and the emotion. During the Embrace practice, we fill this space with our own love and compassion.

The Mindful Gap + Self-Compassion:
Without Mindfulness or Self-Compassion: Critical email from boss (stimulus) –> Amygdala triggers –> React from a place of upset (response) –> Negative consequence at work, and prolonged internal suffering
With Mindfulness: Critical email from boss (stimulus) –> Amygdala triggers, but then is deactivated by mindfulness practice –> **The Mindful Gap** –> Prefrontal cortex is activated –> Respond to boss from a place of reason (response) –> Positive consequence at work, however, we still may be reeling with fear and anger
With Mindfulness and Self-Compassion: Critical email from boss (stimulus) –> Amygdala triggers, but then is deactivated by mindfulness practice –> **The Mindful Gap** –> Prefrontal cortex is activated –> Respond to boss from a place of reason (response) –> Positive consequence at work –> Offer Self-Compassion –> Our emotions of fear and anger are soothed by our own compassion

Tools for Forgiveness

Human development professor and leading self-compassion researcher Kristin Neff, Ph.D., says that self-compassion is not selfish and it can help us to forgive. In her book *Self-Compassion: The Proven Power of Being Kind to Yourself,* Neff explains that when we are more understanding and caring toward ourselves, we can feel this same level of compassion for others. When we have tended to our own challenging feelings, we have a larger bandwidth to help others since we are not absorbed in our internal struggles.

In my experience, after doing self-compassion practices, I not only became more compassionate toward myself but also toward others. I was creating the habit of offering compassion (rather than judgment) for my thoughts and emotions, and recognized that many of them stemmed from childhood wounds. Over time, I began to recognize when others were also behaving from their wounding, and due to my practice, I naturally began to offer compassion for them, as well.

Mindfulness and compassion also help us with forgiveness. When we take the point of view of the observer, we are able to reframe the original situation and see it from a new, wiser perspective. By adding compassion toward ourselves and the other person involved, we are better able to forgive.

For example, when my father left the family, I was only five years old. Being so young, I inaccurately made his absence mean that I wasn't good enough in some way. Today, when the emotion of shame arises, I can observe the feeling and view the original situation with my father more clearly, from a more mature point of view. I now understand that my father's neglect had nothing to do with me—he was doing his best and would have treated any five-year-old in the same way.

This understanding prompts the healing process of the childhood wound, the feeling of shame begins to dissolve, and forgiveness comes naturally. With mindfulness, we see the past with greater clarity, enabling us to create new patterns of patience and understanding. With self-compassion, I can comfort my inner five-year-old and reassure her that she *is* enough, and I would never abandon her.

There is a Buddhist saying: "Holding on to anger is like grasping a hot coal with the intent of throwing it at someone else, but you are the one who gets burned." Even if we are not ready to forgive our worst enemy, practicing mindfulness and compassion can be steps toward forgiveness, which is ultimately an act of self-love.

Feel It to Heal It

In both Buddhist philosophy and Western psychology, there is the belief that past wounds are stored in our bodies. We can heal these wounds if we fully experience the emotions stored within them. As Rumi wrote, "The cure for the pain is in the pain."

Emotions are a combination of physical sensations and the stories we tell ourselves. Emotions live in our bodies and continue to cause suffering until we focus on them directly, which brings their energy to the surface where they can be released.

Emotions and their associated wounds can be healed by bringing mindful awareness, acceptance, and compassion to the emotion. With the Label practice, we identify the emotion. With the Observe practice, we locate it in the physical body and then bring steady attention to it. During the Value practice, we bring awareness to any stories, beliefs, or patterns that may be linked to this emotion. With this greater awareness, these patterns are reframed with wisdom, and subsequently dissolve.[2]

Metamorphosis can often be a painful experience. Therefore, many people keep their pain bottled up inside. If a challenging emotion begins to emerge, many people turn to alcohol, drugs, food, or another addiction to numb or distract themselves.

Although it's easier to keep painful emotions locked up, if we never tend to them, they can persist in our psyche and reveal themselves when we become triggered. For example, residual anger in our bodies can cause us to lash out at a loved one, or pent-up fear could lead to the inability to take risks in life. We often return to our addictions long after these painful events, and the unconscious cycle continues—potentially for a lifetime.

Mindfulness and self-compassion practices offer an alternative to this cycle to feel better and promote healing. Rather than numbing or distracting ourselves, we can allow our challenging emotions to emerge fully and meet them with kindness and compassion. When we are willing to feel painful emotions and hold them with compassion, they are often soothed and less likely to determine our mood or dictate our lives.

Mindfulness and self-compassion practices work together to heal our wounds. Mindfulness serves as the steady beam of awareness that holds the safe container for the challenging emotion to arise. Adding self-compassion provides the courage to face our fears, along with the love and kindness to heal the wound at its root.[3]

It is helpful to remember that emotions are energies in motion, and therefore they are temporary and have a natural cycle. It can be challenging to withstand the pain of the emotion through the entire cycle, but self-compassion provides the strength to stay present while witnessing the emotion rise, linger in the body, and eventually fade away.

In the light of mindful awareness, layers of past hurt, fear, or anger can begin to rise, play themselves out, and then be dispelled from the body. When we are free from the pain of our past, we can meet our present experiences with more clarity, aliveness, and love.

What We Embrace, Dissolves

Psychoanalyst Carl Jung said, "What we resist, persists; embrace it, and it will dissolve." This quote is related to the practice of mindfulness. When we embrace our negative thoughts and emotions with kindness they typically relax. When we allow our charged thoughts and emotions to be as they are and hold loving space for them, they usually soften.

Sometimes, when we put our full attention onto an emotion, it disappears altogether. When we meet the emotion with acceptance and kindness rather than judgment, the emotion integrates into our psyche and dissolves. It's almost as if the resistance to the emotion is what keeps it in place.

This phenomenon occurs because when we perceive something as a problem, the thinking mind latches on and relentlessly tries to fix, manage, and control it. And since the thinking mind is continually working to figure it out, the problem sticks around. What we focus on expands; therefore, our attention on what we *don't* want amplifies the unwanted situation.

For example, if we are single but have a desire to be in partnership, sometimes our focus on "not wanting to be single" is what perpetuates the circumstance. If we view our single status as a "problem," our thinking mind will work diligently to "fix" the problem. Even if we aren't consciously deliberating about it, the thinking mind will continue to toil away, creating low-levels of chronic anxiety and despair.

Although we don't have control over the thinking mind continually trying to fix, manage, and control everything in our lives, we do have control over what we deem as a "problem." We can tell our thinking mind, "*This* is a problem, but this *isn't* a problem." And we can use mindfulness as our tool of discernment.

The Physiology of Self-Compassion

Not only does self-compassion improve our mental health, but it also has measurable effects on our physiology. When we offer compassionate thoughts and emotions to ourselves, the feel-good hormone oxytocin is released, leading to feelings of trust, calm, safety, and connectedness. This improvement in our mood increases our ability to feel warmth and compassion for ourselves.

Self-criticism has the opposite effect on the body. When we criticize ourselves, the amygdala becomes active, and the fight-or-flight response is triggered. Since the amygdala is one of the oldest parts of the brain, it's not able to discern whether the critical thought came from ourselves or someone else. Therefore, it perceives the critical thought as a threat and sends signals to increase blood pressure, adrenaline, and the stress hormone cortisol. Therefore, the inner critic not only affects our mental health, but also our physical health.

A research study conducted by Dr. Kristin Neff found that cortisol levels decreased in response to images that conveyed compassion. When participants used self-compassion practices to soothe their painful emotions, cortisol levels decreased and oxytocin levels increased. Simply by shifting from thoughts of stress to compassion, participants changed the chemical composition of their bodies. Neff's research shows that self-compassion reduces anxiety and depression and softens the impact of adverse events in our lives.[4]

It's helpful to know how oxytocin is produced in the brain since this chemical is associated with wellbeing. Oxytocin is a neurotransmitter that is released when there is loving touch exchanged, such as while hugging a dear friend. When we give or receive a soft, tender caress, oxytocin is released, and we feel at ease.

The release of oxytocin is a response to any caring touch, even when we hug ourselves. The body doesn't discern whether the contact is from a friend or ourselves; it responds to the physical gesture of warmth, love, and care. When we notice when we are becoming stressed, we can tap into this self-healing system by offering ourselves a gentle hug or softly stroking the inside of the forearm.

Just as a loving parent holds and soothes their child during a time of suffering, we can tap into our natural mammalian-caregiving system and hold ourselves. When we ease our own pain with kind words and offer ourselves a caring hug, oxytocin is released, and we feel better—the physiological process is the same.[5]

We can perceive the challenging emotions that arise within us as our wounded inner child. When the intense emotion emerges, it becomes an opportunity to offer compassion to our younger self and heal these wounds. Perhaps as a child, we felt disrespected, abandoned, or neglected. When we practice self-compassion, oxytocin is released and elicits feelings of safety, trust, and connection that the inner child is craving and crying out for.

When we practice, we don't need to understand the whole story in which the wound was originally created. We can detach the story and focus our loving awareness onto the emotion itself. When the compassionate mind shines its light onto the challenging feeling, it transforms the emotion into compassion. When we cultivate our compassionate mind, we hone the skill of alchemizing our suffering into love.

As adults, many of us try to forget the painful memories of our childhood. But by allowing them to be expressed within the safe container of LOVEE, we awaken the sweetness of our own compassion. Rather than becoming bitter about painful events in our lives, we can process challenging emotions with our practice and wrap our pain with love.

We become a compassionate presence that can tenderly hold the rising and passing waves of our own suffering. We become the kind mother that has the strength to carry it all, enabling us to move through the ups and downs of life with immense power and grace.

Cultivating the Compassionate Mind

In the Label and Observe practices, we learned how to distinguish between the "thinking mind" and the "observing mind." Now, with the Embrace practice, we begin to cultivate the "compassionate mind."

The compassionate mind is essentially the observing mind with the addition of compassion. It is the consciousness that embraces our challenging thoughts and emotions with the healing powers of love and kindness.

During meditation, we can identify the various "minds" in our heads, such as:

- The Inner Critic (*Why do you have to be sad all the time?*)
- The "What if…?" Worrying Mind (*What if I don't survive the surgery?*)
- The Victim (*Why do bad things always happen to me?*)
- The Voice of Reason (*You're in good hands with these doctors.*)
- The Compassionate Mind (*This is a hard time, sweetheart, be gentle with yourself. I'm here for you.*)

The compassionate mind is the aspect of consciousness that loves and accepts ourselves unconditionally. And unfortunately, it's typically the quietest voice in our heads.

During my cancer treatments, I knew that practicing loving self-talk was essential for my healing, so I made a concerted effort to cultivate my compassionate mind. I continually checked in with myself and redirected my mind from fearful thinking to thoughts of optimism and hope.

For example, when my mind began to spin due to fear about an upcoming treatment, I'd elicit the compassionate mind and say to myself, *I love myself too much to get on that fearful train of thought. What is the most self-loving thought I can have right now?*

We can also grow the compassionate mind in formal meditation. By repeating kind phrases in our minds, we cultivate a loving attitude toward ourselves. While in seated meditation, we can say to ourselves the following loving-kindness phrases:

- May I be safe and peaceful.
- May I be free from suffering.
- May I be kind to myself.
- May I accept myself just as I am.

Repeating these phrases during my morning meditation, I created an antidote to the inner critic and cultivated feelings of wellbeing that I was able to draw upon later in the day when difficulties arose.

Rather than being so hard on ourselves, we can create new habits of meeting our thoughts and emotions with kindness and compassion. We know that, neurologically, what fires together, wires together. So, over time, we can rewire the brain so that whenever suffering arises, the compassionate mind automatically comes online.

The Embrace Practice Meditation

Listen to the meditation online at:
www.meditationforbreastcancer.com

Find yourself in a comfortable position. Sitting up tall, bring one hand to your heart and one hand to your abdomen. Close your eyes and take three deep breaths in and out through the nose. Bring your focus to the rise and fall of the chest. Allowing the body to soften, allowing the mind to settle.

I invite you to bring to mind a situation in your life that is causing you stress. Locate the stress in the body, perhaps there is tension in the shoulders, the chest or the abdomen. Bringing both hands to your heart, take in a deep breath. Acknowledge what you're going through. Say to yourself, *This is a hard time and it's okay to feel upset. I'm offering myself some kindness and compassion.* Feel the soothing touch of your hands on your heart.

Open your hands in front of you in the shape of a cup. Keeping your eyes closed, label your emotion—such as anger, anxiety or depression—and then imagine this emotion as energy in your hands. Get curious about this emotion. What does it look like? What color it is? Is it moving, fast or slow?

As if you were speaking to a little child that is suffering, tend to this emotion with love and care. Bring your hands to your heart as if you are embracing this little one, offering the emotion a loving embrace. Say to the emotion, *I see you, sweetheart, I hear you, I love you, and I've got you. You are safe with me. You are safe here.*

Now ask the emotion, *What do you need right now, sweetheart? What do you need?*

And then, listen, with an open heart. Once you've received what your emotion needs, just like a loving parent, offer it what it needs right now. *You need love? I love you. You need safety? You are always safe with me. You need respect? I will always honor, appreciate, and respect you.*

Continue offering words of compassion for this emotion, saying the phrases that your little one needs to hear right now, such as:

- I will always see your goodness.
- I will always hold you with loving-kindness.
- I will never leave you. I will always be here for you.
- I will always support you. I will always believe in you.
- You are always welcome here. You can stay as long as you need.
- You are safe. You can rest in my heart.

Continue breathing, embracing, and offering kindness. Savoring the comfort, the sweetness, and the love that we feel when we offer ourselves compassion.

As you embrace the emotion with tenderness, you may feel the energy of the emotion begin to relax and transform. As if the emotion was one drop of water, you may feel it dissolve into the ocean of the compassionate mind. Your emotion becomes integrated into the pure light of your loving awareness.

Take in a deep breath. Give yourself a big hug, holding onto your opposite shoulders and gently swaying left and right. Remember, during challenging times in life, we can hold ourselves. Take in one last deep breath, and gently release the arms on the exhale, and when you're ready, slowly open your eyes.

Part 5
"E" is for Equanimity

Chapter 13
Welcome to Pure Land

"You never know how strong you are until being strong is the only choice you have."
Bob Marley, singer-songwriter

Saying Good-bye

It was October 24, 2018, the night before my major surgery. Three procedures would take place the next day: removal and biopsy of my right breast (while keeping the skin intact); fat transfer from my stomach to reconstruct a new breast; removal and biopsy of nine lymph nodes from my right arm. My two surgeons, Dr. Kusske and Dr. Roostaeian would tag team—once Dr. Kusske was complete with the mastectomy, Dr. Roostaeian would take over for the reconstruction.

My nervous system was hijacked with fear. I took a bath to try and relax. But in the bathtub, I had a clear view of my right breast. I looked down, tilted my head and thought, *I'm so sorry. I have to say good-bye to you tomorrow*. I began to weep tears of grief.

It's not like I was having knee-replacement surgery; I was losing a body part tied to my femininity, beauty, and identity as a woman. With so much uncertainty about the outcome of these procedures, my mind began to spiral in fear, *How painful is this going to be? Will there be complications? What if I don't wake up from the surgery?*

I quickly started to spiral down a dark hole of fear and I needed help. I got out of the bathtub, put on a robe, and texted my meditation teacher.

"Hi, Heather, can you talk? I have my surgery tomorrow," I texted.

A second later, the phone rang.

"Hi Sharon, dear," Heather said. "How are you doing?"

"I'm not doing well," I said. "My surgery is tomorrow, and I'm terrified."

"Oh, sweetheart, of course you are," she said, reassuringly. "It's all going to be okay."

"Okay," I said, shaking. "Thank you for spending this time with me."

"Remember that you are a part of Pure Land where everything is happening *for* you, everything is unfolding exactly as it should," she said. "Now is the time to breathe and deepen your faith."

"Okay," I said, taking several deep breaths. "What is Pure Land?"

"Pure Land is the true nature of reality," she said. "The veils of the thinking mind and the ego are lifted, and we see clearly that we are all the same light at our core, we experience the deep understanding that we are all interconnected."

"That is so beautiful," I said. My mind and body started to relax.

"In Pure Land, when you look at a tree, you don't just see the tree. You see that it offers us oxygen, and we offer it carbon dioxide," she said. "The earth is our mother embracing us with its gravity. The sky is our father, a gentle blanket of love and protection."

"Yes, I understand," I said with a slight smile.

"When we walk down the street, we are walking as bodies of light, not as physical bodies," she said. "I walk as my pure body, the part of me that is pure light, the Buddha nature within me, the part of me that cannot be sick. When we look at each other, we don't see our physical bodies, and we don't see illness—we only see our light bodies and acknowledge that in Spirit, we are one."

"Yes, I can see that, I can feel that connection," I said. My eyes were closed, and my heart was open to the blissful experience of Pure Land.

"Tomorrow, imagine that the hospital is Pure Land," she said. "That all the nurses and doctors are buddhas and bodhisattvas there to help you and there for your optimal healing. And remember that you are deeply held and deeply loved. You are protected, sweetheart."

"Thank you, Heather, I will remember," I said, tears of gratitude welling up in my eyes. "This was so helpful."

"You're very welcome," she said. "Sweet dreams."

The Fateful Day

The next morning, my alarm went off at 4:00 a.m. With a firm commitment to staying positive, I said to myself, *Today, I choose to have thoughts of peace, trust, and gratitude. Today, I am in Pure Land.* I took a deep breath into that intention.

It had been six months since my diagnosis, and I had been strengthening my mind every day with mindfulness practices. Today marked the pinnacle of my treatments, the grand finale. I had been in ninja-mindset training for six months, and today was the main event that I'd been training for.

Mom picked me up at 4:30 a.m. and drove me to the hospital. "How are you feeling?" she asked.

"I'm okay," I said. "You know, I'm just going to sit back and let the doctors do their jobs." Mom smiled, appreciating my strength.

We parked, and the two of us walked up the street in silence. We turned the corner and looked up at the Ronald Reagan UCLA Medical Center as the sun was starting to rise.

I raised my arms into the air and said, "Welcome to Pure Land!"

Mom gave me a quizzical look. "What does that mean?"

"Pure Land is a Buddhist concept. Heather shared it with me last night," I said. "It's the acknowledgment that we are all connected. It's heaven on earth."

"That's beautiful," said Mom. "But why is the hospital Pure Land?"

"I typically see hospitals as places of science. Yes, people are here to help, but it's kind of a sterile factory churning out patients," I said. "But today, I need something more comforting to get me through the day. So I'm going to use my imagination and see the hospital as Pure Land, a land of light, purity, and grace."

"I think that's a wonderful idea," Mom said.

As we walked through the doors of the hospital, a rush of energy came toward me. Doctors, nurses, and patients were scurrying around. I imagined all of the health-care workers as bodhisattvas. When I looked at patients, I didn't see their illness, I saw their light bodies. I saw them already healed.

We checked in with the bodhisattva at the front desk. "Good morning, Sharon," she said with a relaxed smile and handed me a clipboard of papers. "Have a seat. Let's get you checked in."

"Thank you," I said. I took a seat and started filling out the paperwork.

At 5:30 a.m., I said good-bye to Mom in the waiting room, walked into a patient room, and changed into a gown. A nurse was asking me questions when my two surgeons, Dr. Kusske and Dr. Roostaeian, walked by the doorway.

As if I'd caught a glimpse of A-list celebrities, I sat up quickly and thought to myself, *My Buddhas are here!*

"Hiii!" I said to them, with fan-girl excitement. They waved and smiled at me.

"Hi, Sharon! We will be right back," said Dr. Kusske. I felt a wave of safety come over me. I was in good hands.

A few more nurses came in to greet me and tell me their roles in the procedure. Soon after, my breast surgeon, Dr. Kusske, came into the room.

"Good morning, Sharon. How are you feeling today?" she asked.

"I feel good," I said. "I'm grateful that you're the one doing this today."

"Well, I'm sure it will go just fine," she said reassuringly.

As Dr. Kusske left, the plastic surgeon Dr. Roostaeian came in.

"Hi, Sharon," he said with a smile. "How are you feeling?"

"I feel good," I said. "I'm ready."

He held up a red marker and said, "I just need to draw a few marks on you."

As the doctor drew red lines on my abdomen and right breast, marking where he would later apply a scalpel, I went into a mini-state of shock, and my mind disassociated from my body. To manage the fear, I shifted my perspective and viewed my anatomy as an object going through the cancer-removal process, rather than something personal.

Trust, trust, trust. I thought to myself, taking several deep breaths. *I'm in good hands. This is the path to becoming cancer-free. I'm in Pure Land. I am safe.*

"Okay, you're all set," he said. "Don't worry, today is going to go really smoothly."

I believed him. He was Superman, after all.

As Dr. Roostaeian walked out, the anesthesiologist swooped in. She was a ninety-pound, perky woman who sang like a fairy godmother when she spoke.

"Hellooo, Sharon," she said. "We are going to take you to the operating room now, but first, here is something to make you a little sleepy, then I'll give you the full anesthesia later."

"Okay, thank you," I said.

The nurse laid down my bed and wheeled me into the operating room. Through the IV, I felt a coolness enter my veins, and then everything got a little fuzzy. *Ahhh, Pure Land.*

"Okaaay," the anesthesiologist sang, "the anesthesia is going in now." Click.

"Okaaay, surgery is over," sang the anesthesiologist.

With my eyes closed, I heard beeping and the faint sound of chatter. I slowly opened my eyes to see lights and nurses shuffling around. A nurse looked down at me and began to speak, but I couldn't understand her. It was as if I was in an aquarium, having a fluid, dream-like experience of blurred vision and muffled voices. Although it was a strange feeling, I felt safe, and I fell back asleep.

The Sailboat Returned to Level

The next morning, I woke up and I knew. I knew that I no longer had cancer in my body. I felt the sailboat of my nervous system, which had been at a forty-five-degree tilt of anxiety for six straight months, relax to a level position upon a glassy ocean. I knew I was safe now. Even though my physical body was incapacitated, my nervous system was back to smooth sailing.

I looked around my hospital room.

"Look who's awake," said Mom, who got up from her bed and walked toward mine. She put on some relaxing acoustic guitar music from her iPhone.

"Hi, Mom," I said groggily.

"How are you feeling?" she said.

"I'm okay ... sleepy," I said.

"Well, I have good news to share with you," she said with a huge smile on her face. "After Dr. Kusske completed the mastectomy and removed nine lymph nodes, she did a biopsy and found that *all* of the cancer was gone."

"It's gone?" I asked, with excitement. "It's *all* gone?"

"Yep," said Mom. "The chemo worked so well that it wiped out every single cancer cell, and the biopsy proved it. This also means that you don't need radiation. You're done, honey! You're all done!"

I let that sink in. I was cancer-free! Although I couldn't move my body, I was jumping for joy on the inside. Tears ran down my face, and I whispered, "Mom, we did it. Victory!"

Mom held my hand and looked at me. "*You* did it."

A nurse came into the room and started to check my vitals.

"Hi, Sharon, you're awake," she said. "It's good that you slept for so long. That was an eight-hour surgery, and you'll be here for three more nights. But the surgery went well, there were no complications, and you're recovering just fine."

The surgery was eight *hours long? It felt like one second.*

I was bewildered by the length of the surgery and my experience of time. I had been under anesthesia before, but only for an hour or two. This surgery marked the longest I had ever been unconscious, and to think that it was for eight solid hours was unnerving.

I'll never forget that one moment without consciousness. It felt like a place where space and time did not exist. *Was that where I came from? Was that where I will go after I die? Was I with Spirit for those eight hours?*

As I contemplated the experience of my anesthesia-induced coma, the nurse confirmed that all my vital signs were on point and brought my attention back into the room.

"Everything looks good, Sharon," said the nurse. "I like the music you have on—it's peaceful." The nurse left the room, and I fell back asleep for another ten hours.

The next morning, I woke up to the sound of people marching into the room and surrounding my hospital bed. I blinked open my eyes and saw seven residents, bright-eyed and bushy-tailed, looking down at me. With clipboard and pen in hand, each resident was ready and eager to learn. I looked at the clock—it was 6:00 a.m. on the nose. *How can they be so awake at this hour?*

"Hello, Sharon," said the woman on my right. "We are plastic surgeon residents. We work with Dr. Roostaeian. Do you mind if we take a look?"

I nodded, and she gently pulled down my gown to expose my newly constructed right breast.

"Wow, the shape is perfect," she said under her breath. I smiled and let out a sigh of relief.

The woman on my left started speaking to the group as if she were giving a presentation to the United Nations. The precision with which these residents walked and talked was a sure sign that they would be precise with a scalpel as future surgeons.

"Thank you, Sharon," she said to me. "We will be back tomorrow morning at this same time."

As they marched out of the room like soldiers in unison, I looked at Mom and said, "Impressive."

Then, I fell back asleep.

Working with Pain

The next morning, after the army of residents completed their rounds, I started to feel some pain in my abdomen. The anesthesia from the surgery was starting to wear off. I pressed a button to administer pain medication into my IV, but I knew there would be a forty-five-minute delay until it kicked in.

I recalled what my meditation teacher, Heather, had taught me about working with pain:

"When you feel pain," said Heather, "bring your attention right onto it and label the pain, such as, 'tingling' or 'burning,' and then shift your attention to something that feels good, such as the soft texture of a blanket, and say 'this sensation is here, too.'"

The time had come to follow these instructions. As I began to feel pain in my abdomen, I reached for a soft blanket.

Okay, let me try this meditation. I thought to myself, reluctantly. *Stabbing, stabbing is here,* referring to the pain in my abdomen. *And softness is here too,* shifting my focus to the blanket. *Both sensations are here and I can be with both sensations without reacting to them.*

I was able to shift out of my reluctant mindset and into the present moment by bringing curiosity to the practice. I thought, *What are the qualities of this stabbing sensation? Is it sharp or dull? Is it quick or slow? Is it moving?* When the pain became too much to bear, I shifted my full attention back to the softness of the blanket.

Like a pendulum, I continued the practice, slowly and deliberately placing my attention onto one sensation and then the other. *Stabbing ... softness; Stabbing ... softness.* With each deep breath, I remained even-keeled while observing both ends of this spectrum of sensations.

This pendulum practice helped me to understand the pain for what it actually was—a myriad of sensations in the body that come and go. Since the sensations were always changing, there was no need to react to them, no need to push away the painful one or cling to the soft one. Both sensations were in my present moment experience, and they would both eventually change. I continued to breathe into this knowing that all sensations change.

With each passing minute of practice, I was building my equanimous, nonreactive mind, and growing my capacity to handle the physical pain with grace.

About an hour later, a physical therapist came into my room.

"Hi, Sharon," she said. "It's time to get you up and walking today."

"Oh, okay," I said, grudgingly.

Due to my abdominal procedure, which involved an incision from one hip bone across my abdomen to the other hip bone, walking was difficult and painful. The therapist rolled me over to my side and stood me up. With one hand on my back and one hand on my elbow, she helped me walk into the hallway. Step by step, I moved like I was walking through molasses.

"Great job!" she said, as she walked me back into my room and assisted me down into a chair. We shared some small talk. I asked her if she had any plans for the weekend.

"Well, since tomorrow is Halloween, I'll be going trick-or-treating with my two boys," she said.

"Oh, that's right, Halloween," I said. "I dressed up as Wonder Woman last year. I don't think I'll be dressing up this year."

"Well, you *are* Wonder Woman this year," she said. "We need to get you a cape!"

"Ha, yes," I said. "Sometimes Halloween costumes come true, right?"

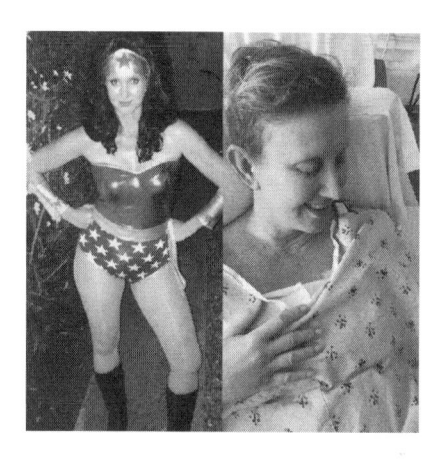

My two versions of Wonder Woman, one year apart.

The therapist helped me back into bed. After a few hours of listening to music and eating a somewhat palatable meal, I fell asleep for the night.

The next morning, the plastic surgeon, Dr. Roostaeian, came in to see if I was strong enough to go home that day. I had spent four nights in the hospital and I was ready to go home. Luckily, after checking my vitals, he cleared me to go.

"Great job!" Dr. Roostaeian said.

"I didn't do anything," I responded. "*You're* the one who did a great job."

"Well, you were a big part of it," he said. "It's *your* body that's doing the healing, and you're doing great."

Working with Physical Pain Meditation

Practice after Surgery

Listen to the meditation online at:
www.meditationforbreastcancer.com

For this meditation, you will need a soft blanket or something that feels pleasant to the touch. May this meditation alleviate some of your suffering and promote healing in the body and mind.

Try to get as comfortable as you can, either lying down or sitting on your cushion or on a chair. Closing the eyes, taking a deep breath, and feeling the connection between your body and the floor or chair beneath you. Relaxing the entire body and feeling the weight of your body fully supported from head to toe.

Allow your facial muscles to relax. Relaxing the forehead, relaxing the cheeks and the eyes. Relaxing all the muscles of the jaw. Breath in deeply, and relax all the muscles of the shoulders, the chest, and the back. Continue taking deep breaths as you relax the chest, your abdomen and all your internal organs. Releasing any tension in the lower back, the hips, the pelvis. Relaxing the thighs, the knees, all the way down to the feet. A wave of relaxation flows from your head down to your feet.

Holding the blanket in one hand, bring your attention to the physical sensations of the blanket. What sensations do you notice? Is it soft? Fuzzy? Cool or warm? Sustain your attention on the blanket for about a minute, really feeling and acknowledging the pleasant sensations.

Now shift your attention to the area of your body where you're feeling pain. Notice and label the sensations of the physical pain. Is it sharp or dull? Burning? Stabbing? If the pain ever becomes too overwhelming, you can always return to the pleasant sensation of the blanket at *any* time during this exercise.

But if you're able, sustain your focus at the site of the pain for twenty seconds, and then shift your attention back to the soft sensation of the blanket. Let yourself stay present and aware of pleasant sensations for the next couple of minutes. Resting your awareness here.

Now we will work with the emotions related to this surgery. What are your thoughts and emotions related to this pain? Do you resent it? Do you feel like someone took something from you? Is there grief, anger, or frustration associated with this pain? Are you afraid of the pain? Do you just wish it would go away?

Take some time to identify and label your thoughts and emotions. Anger is here. Fear is present. Resentment is here. Remember there is nothing good or bad, we are just noticing whatever is here. Take another deep breath and observe whatever thoughts and emotions are present, and simply allow them to be here. Also, remember that you can bring your attention back to the comforting sensation of the blanket at any time.

Now shift your attention back to your physical body. Do you feel any other sensations *associated* with this pain, such as a twisting in the gut or rapid heart rate? Noticing these physical reactions, take another breath, and allow them to be here. After about thirty seconds, gently bring your attention back to the soft sensation of the blanket and rest your mind for a couple of minutes.

When you're ready, bring your full attention back to the painful area in your body. If you can, bring a sense of curiosity to the ever-changing set of sensations. Do the sensations stay in one place or are they moving? Where do they go? Do they get stronger or weaker? Continue to track these sensations for about thirty seconds. Just witnessing, not trying to change anything. Cultivating a nonreactive mind. And now return your attention to the soft sensation of the blanket, and once again rest there for a couple of minutes.

Now for the last time, take another deep breath and return your awareness like a spotlight onto the painful area and sustain your focus for forty seconds, a little bit longer. What do you notice this time? Is the sensation different or the same? Has it moved? Where is it now? Feeling and acknowledging whatever is present in this moment. And now bring your awareness back to the soft sensation of the blanket.

Like a pendulum, shift your focus from the blanket to the painful area and back to the blanket again. Acknowledge the painful sensation by saying, *this is here,* and then shift your attention to the soft blanket and say, and, *this is here, too. This is here, and this is here, too.* Both sensations exist here and now. I can *be* with both sensations without clinging to one or pushing away the other. Simply letting every sensation in our present moment awareness to be here, just as it is.

Now gently place one hand on the painful area in your body and offer it some compassion. Lovingly say to the pain, *I see that you're hurting and I'm sorry. This is a hard time. I love you, and I'll take good care of you.* After holding the painful area with compassion, notice what happens to the sensations. If nothing changes, that is perfectly fine, too. Bring your hand back to your lap and bring your attention to the whole body. Bring your attention to the whole body.

As we bring our meditation to a close, notice how you're feeling. How is your body feeling? Feel the connection between your body and the chair or the floor beneath you. Begin gentle movements of the body. Wiggle your fingers and your toes. Take another deep breath and exhale out the mouth. Whenever you're ready, gently open your eyes.

Chapter 14
Strength Through Surrender

"Surrender is the ultimate sign of strength and the foundation for a spiritual life. Surrender is a gift that you can give yourself."
Debbie Ford, spiritual teacher

The Natural Healing Intelligence of the Body

As Mom drove me home from the hospital, I thought about what Dr. Roostaeian had said—that *I* was the one doing the healing of my body, not the doctors or nurses. This idea perplexed me because all I was doing was sleeping, but after some thought, I began to understand what he meant. As the medical team created the pathway, it was the natural intelligence of *my* body that did the healing. By creating the right environment, the cells of my body knew how to regenerate spontaneously.

Due to my scientific background, I understood the physiology of healing. In our bodies, the autonomic nervous system manages our automatic functions, such as the heartbeat, and it's the system that is related to how we respond to stress. The autonomic nervous system has two branches: the sympathetic nervous system (known as the fight-or-flight mode) and the parasympathetic nervous system (the rest-and-digest or healing mode).

When we experience a perceived threat, the sympathetic nervous system kicks in, causing a cascade of biological signals to help us fight or escape the danger. For example, when we are scared, the heart starts pounding, the breath rate increases and adrenaline is pumped into the bloodstream to boost our strength and energy.

When the sympathetic nervous system is in charge, healing doesn't occur in the body. So I knew it was crucial for my recovery to calm my fearful mind and shift my nervous system from the sympathetic to the parasympathetic. Luckily, I had my mindfulness practices to do just that.

When we arrived at my house, Mom helped me out of the car and walked me to my bedroom. I caught myself in the mirror and stopped to look. My skin was pale with a greenish tint. I unzipped my robe to reveal bandages on my right breast and abdomen, along with four plastic tubes coming out of my body. These tubes were drains that needed to be cleaned out every couple of hours. I was horrified by the vision of my body. I looked like a gruesome creature out of a science-fiction movie.

I shuffled to my bed and laid down. Even though my mind was filled with thoughts of self-judgment, fear, and anger, I closed my eyes and remembered my promise to stay positive. I said to myself, *Trust the process. This too shall pass. I am safe, I surrender, and I allow my body to heal.*

By offering mindfulness and compassion to my fearful thoughts, I cultivated a mental state of surrender. With slow deep breaths, elongating the exhale, my mind began to relax and my nervous system shifted from the sympathetic into the parasympathetic. I fell into a deep sleep and allowed my body's natural healing intelligence to work its magic throughout the night.

Who Am I?

The next morning, my body felt like it had been hit by a truck. The intense heaviness in my body felt like weights holding me down on my bed. My stomach growled with hunger and I instinctively crunched my abs to sit up.

"Ooouch," I yelped.

It became clear that sitting up on my own was not happening. I called Mom, who was in the next room.

"Hey, Mom, can you help me up?" I said, completely frustrated and ashamed of my lack of independence.

"Of course, angel," she said, walking into my bedroom.

Mom rolled my body slowly to the side of the bed, helped me to stand up, and walked me to the kitchen.

Although I was cancer-free and my fear of death was relieved, I was now confronted with a new set of challenges. I had always identified as an athlete, as well as being independent and resourceful, so needing help to walk was particularly frustrating. I felt weak. I couldn't "power" through it, so I needed to cultivate yet another way of being—*humility*.

During breakfast, my mind began to whirl. *What if my body doesn't heal correctly? What if I never get sensation in my right breast and abdomen? What if my breast looks weird and my torso is too scarred that no man would be attracted to me again?*

I thought I would be in a constant state of happiness to be cancer-free, but that was not the case. My oncologist warned that after being medically cleared, many women have a dip emotionally, and grief, in particular, can set in. Her words made sense to me now.

Since cancer treatment was relentless—it was essentially one traumatic experience after the other—there was no time to process during the span of treatment. Having poison put into someone's bloodstream would be the single most horrible thing in one person's life, but a cancer patient goes through this *multiple* times, not to mention the removal of a sex organ from the body.

Since my nervous system had been in fight-or-flight for a sustained amount of time, it could take several weeks before it adjusted back to equilibrium. If I were living during the Stone Age, it would be as if a lion had been chasing me for six straight months, and then abruptly stopped. Since I no longer feared for my life, I suddenly had the space to feel the various emotions that I'd been accumulating. The first day I was declared cancer-free was the first day I could stop and think, *What the hell just happened?*

My doctor was right—the grief that filled my body was overwhelming. Although I had my life, I had lost many things due to this journey. My once strong body that trekked mountains and completed triathlons was now bedridden. My once long wavy hair was now an inch long and paper-thin. My once unmarred abdomen and right breast were now injured and scarred. I did not feel powerful or beautiful whatsoever. My sense of identity was derailed.

Like a wounded animal, I stumbled back into my bed and curled up in a ball of self-pity. I'd known that recovery from surgery would be tough physically, but I hadn't anticipated it to be this difficult emotionally and psychologically.

While lying in bed, I thought back to the time I spent a month at an ashram in India. I was studying the yoga philosophy of Vedanta, and one of the key teachings was to ask the question, *Who am I?*

At the ashram, the teacher asked the students these questions:

"Who are you? What do you identify with? Are you the car that you drive? Are you your job? Are you the number in your bank account? Are you someone's spouse? Are you someone's parent? Are you the size of the pants that you wear? Are you your physical beauty? Are you some kind of personality trait, such as 'friendly' or 'smart'?"

My teacher paused to allow time for contemplation.

"All of those things—material things, the amount of money you have, relationships, your physical body, your mental capacity—are all subject to the law of impermanence. They are always changing, so if you are attached to them, you will experience suffering when they inevitably change. And can you be something that is always changing? How can you identify with something that is a moving target?"

Another pause.

"Who are you at your core? Connect with the part of you that does not change. This is who you are. This is your identity."

I realized that it wasn't until now that I *actually* was doing this contemplation practice. When I was at the ashram, I was 32 years old, strong and healthy. So, it was easy for me to say, "I am not my body, I am my Spirit." Now, lying in the fetal position on my bed, it was much more difficult to say those words. It wasn't until my strength and beauty were compromised that I realized I'd been taking them for granted all along.

I took out my journal and started writing to help me discover a new identity, a new normal. I wrote:

Who am I? What key aspects of my identity are currently compromised?

1. Being an athlete: Previous to my diagnosis, I lifted weights three times a week and did yoga almost every day. Now I was hunched over and couldn't even walk a block without getting tired. If I wasn't going for a run or doing a yoga class, then who was I?

2. Being a yogini: Previous to my diagnosis, I took pride in being pharmaceutical-free and utilizing yoga, breathwork, meditation, and healthy food as my medicine. But throughout chemotherapy and during surgery recovery, I was taking upwards of ten pills per day. If I wasn't a yogini, then who was I?

3. Being a woman: I previously felt feminine with long hair, natural breasts, and an unscarred body. Now my hair was an inch long, and my stomach and right breast were healing from surgery. My hair would grow back, but the scars would remain. If I didn't have long hair and an unscarred body, then who was I? What was the definition of being an attractive woman? What makes a woman beautiful?

4. Being a potential mother: I'd previously had regular periods, but chemotherapy put me into premature menopause. I had frozen my eggs, but would if that didn't work? Would a man still love me if I couldn't bear his children? Was I defective now in some way? If I no longer had the vision of being a mother in the future, then who was I?

With quiet tears, I put down my journal and sat down on my meditation pillow to do my practice. I labeled the emotion, "Grief. Grief is here." I observed the energy of grief swirl around in my body and it became concentrated in my heart. I valued the notion that I was not alone in feeling grief and that other women going through cancer treatment were going through these same losses. I brought my hands to my heart, embracing the grief, offering it as much love and compassion as I could muster.

When the grief began to fade, and the tears began to subside, I asked myself, *With all of these layers pulled away, what is left? Who are you, Sharon?*

It became clear that I was the part of me that could never get sick; the part of me that never changes; the part of me that will live on after my body perishes. As if being in a chrysalis wrapped in these false identities, once I realized that each identity was an illusion, the chrysalis began to expand. Metamorphosis was happening, and these truths became clear:

It was my Spirit, not my body, that defined my strength.
It was my Spirit, not my physical traits, that defined my beauty.
It was my Spirit, not external circumstances, that created my happiness.

My identity became crystal clear—*I am my Spirit.*

I was not a human having a spiritual experience; I was a Spirit having a human experience, and this experience with cancer was far and away the wildest one yet.

Resistance Causes Suffering

The next day, the sun was out, the birds were singing and I wanted to go outside and enjoy the beautiful day.

"Ugh, I hate this," I said, as I rolled over in pain. I was not only resisting the physical pain, but also the fact that I would be bedridden for the next few days.

Mom came into my room, "Are you okay?"

"No, this really sucks," I said. "How long do I need to stay in bed?"

"Maybe about a week?" Mom said. I cringed and rolled over to the other side.

"You need patience, honey. That's why they call you a patient," Mom said with a smile. "Healing takes time. You just need to rest."

Mom's words were reassuring. As she left my room, I realized that I was once again throwing the second arrow by resisting my condition. I remembered that when I resisted, I suffered. So, the best way to release my suffering was to let go of control and accept that my body would heal in its own time.

I closed my eyes and repeated the mindfulness phrase of acceptance, *Things are as they are, may I accept things just as they are.*

After about five minutes of repeating this phrase, my resistance began to fall away and I felt more relaxed. This phrase helped me to let go of the fight. In this mental state of acceptance, I was no longer suffering.

In his book *The Mindful Path to Self-Compassion*, clinical psychologist Christopher Germer shared this formula to explain the concept that resistance directly causes suffering:

Pain x Resistance = Suffering

In this formula, "Pain" is not referring to physical pain. "Pain" is the unavoidable hardship in life, such as receiving a cancer diagnosis. "Resistance" is any reaction to ward off the pain, such as tensing the body or complaining about wanting the pain to go away. "Suffering" is the physical and emotional tension that we add to the pain with resistance, layer upon layer.

This formula took what I'd previously learned about pain and suffering to the next level. It helped me realize that I could avoid suffering *altogether* by releasing resistance, or my negative reaction to the pain.

Once again, I would have to apply this wisdom to help me cope: *It is not the circumstance that causes suffering; it is my resistance to the circumstance that causes me to suffer.*

According to the formula, the more I resisted being bedridden, the more I would suffer; and there was the possibility of *zero* suffering if I surrendered *all* resistance:

Pain x 0 = 0

This awareness made me realize that suffering was a choice. At any moment that I was suffering, I could ask myself, *What am I resisting? What do I wish was different?*

If I couldn't do anything about the given problem, I could drop into a state of acceptance by repeating the phrase: *Things are as they are, may I accept things just as they are.*

Although it seemed counter intuitive, I discovered that when I fully accepted my circumstances—when I fully surrendered to whatever was happening—I felt a sense of strength. It was empowering to know that although bad things would continue to happen in life, I always had the choice whether or not I suffered.

A Miracle on the Venice Canals

A few days after I returned home from the hospital was Halloween. As the sun set, I peered out my living room window to see children dressed in costumes, walking from one house to another. Even though I turned off my porch light, a few trick-or-treaters still rang my doorbell. I contemplated opening the door and flashing the kids my grotesque fluid-filled drains coming out of my body (Halloween was supposed to be scary, right?), but I didn't want to scare the poor children. At least I had a good laugh about how solid my costume was—I certainly would have won "scariest" in any contest.

The next morning marked one week since surgery. I was excited to get outside and take a walk on along the canals of Venice, a little beach town in Los Angeles. It was on this walk that I had the most spiritually profound experience of my cancer journey.

While strolling the canals, I continued to repeat the acceptance phrase, *Things are as they are; may I accept things just as they are.*

Since having cancer was the hardest thing I'd ever had to accept, I had been repeating this phrase every single day since diagnosis. Since it had been six months of this daily practice, the neurons of my brain had shifted to create a new mindset of acceptance, but not just about my health— about *everything* in my life.

Due to neuroplasticity, my default state of mind was slowly shifting from having a constant craving that things were different, to a more equanimous experience of ease, peace, and contentment.

As a result of six months of repeating this phrase, something clicked and I completely let go. From the state of my physical body, to my finances, to my marital or motherhood statuses, I let go of the misery of chronically wanting things to be different. I let go of the stories I had created around not having certain things. I let go of thinking there was something wrong with me for not having them. I let go of the "wanting mind" that needed something more, something different than what was right here and right now.

As I stood on the canals admiring the ripples on the water, I realized that this was the first time in my life that I didn't wish that *something* was different. Although my current life circumstances were certainly worse than in the past, since I had cultivated nonreactivity with my consistent practices, I had relaxed into the most profound state of acceptance than I'd ever experienced before.

I closed my eyes and again repeated the phrase, *Things are as they are; I accept everything in my life exactly as it is in this moment.*

Then something unexpected happened. As if doing a spring cleaning of my psyche, this practice cleared out all the cluttered feelings of craving, frustration, and resentment that had been taking space in my subconscious. From this clearing of the psyche, I dropped fully into the present moment and experienced an expansive feeling of spaciousness in my body and a luminous presence in my heart.

I was liberated from the chattering mind and the constant feelings of worry and discontent, and I touched into a profound silence within. From this void, joy and gratitude spontaneously arose and filled my being completely.

I opened my eyes and looked around the canals. The trees came alive, the colors of the flowers became more vibrant, and the sunlight glistening on the water looked like diamonds. It was an experience so beautiful and intense that I fell to my knees in tears.

Once again, I was overwhelmed, but not by fear. This time I was overwhelmed with gratitude for the beauty that was right in front of me. This beauty had been there all along; I just hadn't entirely seen it before since I was distracted by my thoughts and constantly wishing that something was different.

Sitting on the bank of the canal, the loving presence in my heart expanded in all directions. The boundaries between my body, the trees, the flowers, and the water became fluid, and I experienced a profound feeling of oneness with all of life.

I closed my eyes, began to meditate, and savored this sensation of deep interconnection. I was experiencing the true nature of reality—*that we are all one in Spirit and separation is an illusion.*

After about thirty minutes of meditation, I opened my eyes, took a deep breath, and smiled with satisfaction.

On my way home, I reveled in the feelings of joy and gratitude. I had written gratitude journals in the past, but I'd never before experienced the level of gratitude that I felt that afternoon. I realized that if I were resisting anything in my life, I could not experience gratitude fully—I could not feel resistance and gratitude at the same time.

So rather than doing a gratitude journal, which felt like an attempt to *force* gratitude, I could dissolve resistance by repeating the acceptance phrase—*Things are as they are, may I accept things just as they are*—and then joy and gratitude would arise effortlessly.

That hour on the Venice Canals shifted my consciousness forever. Now I knew what was possible. Now I understood, first hand, the experience of divine presence and the interconnection of all of life. Now I knew that acceptance and complete surrender to life were the gateways to divine bliss, enduring strength, and the feeling of being fully alive.

Connecting with nature on the Venice Canals.

Healing Visualization Meditation

Practice after Surgery

Listen to the meditation online at:
www.meditationforbreastcancer.com

Find yourself in a comfortable position, either laying down on your bed or seated on a chair. Imagine that your body is immersed in a golden healing light. This beautiful light fills the feet and legs, then moves into the abdomen and chest and through the arms, then up the neck and out the top of your head. Feeling this golden light swirling up through the body, reorganizing the cells in a new and healthier way. Your entire body radiates with wellbeing.

Bring your attention to your chest and imagine golden light emanating from your heart and infusing your breast tissue. Every cell in the breasts is bathed and blessed by this healing light. Trusting and allowing the natural intelligence of the body to heal you effortlessly. Let yourself be cared for by your own loving presence.

Rest in the knowing that your breast tissue knows exactly what it needs to do to harmonize with their new, healthier state. The cells of the breasts already know that all is well. The cancer has been removed and dissolved. In the breasts and in the entire body, there is only health and wellbeing.

As you are healing, every layer of the body—physical, mental, emotional, and spiritual—is metamorphosing. Your body's recovery from surgery is a part of this transformation process. Your emotions coming up are part of the process of you shedding your layers so that your new, more powerful, more beautiful Self emerges. Allow that to happen now. The metamorphosis is happening.

You are right where you're supposed to be. All is well on every level of your being. All you need to do is rest and trust that as long as the mind is calm and the body is relaxed, the body already knows what to do in order to heal.

Deep relaxation is happening now as divine intelligence of healing light washes through the body. Feeling a sense of wholeness and optimal health in this relaxed state. Letting the body know that it's done a great job through the process of surgery. Now it's time to rest, renew, and rejuvenate.

Bring one hand to your heart and one hand to your abdomen, and give yourself a gentle hug. Breath in and out slowly and sweetly, offering your body so much love and compassion during this tender time. Be gentle with yourself. Be kind with yourself. Remember that you are loved deeply.

As we bring our meditation to a close, notice how you're feeling. How is your body feeling? Feel the connection between your body and the chair or the floor beneath you. Begin gentle movements of the body. Wiggle your fingers and your toes. Bring a gentle smile to your face, knowing that all is well, and your body will heal in its own time. And when you're ready, take one last deep breath, and gently open your eyes.

Chapter 15

The Equanimity Practice—Accept the Situation

"The curious paradox is that when I accept myself just as I am, then I can change."
Carl Rogers, psychologist

What Is Equanimity and Why Is It Important?

Although equanimity is not a word we use in everyday language, it's foundational for our happiness and wellbeing. *Merriam-Webster's Collegiate Dictionary* defines equanimity as "evenness of mind, especially under stress." I define equanimity as inner strength and emotional resilience—which is why it is the final practice, and the ultimate goal, of The LOVEE Method.

Equanimity means having a state of mind that is at ease, balanced, and nonreactive. To be reactive means acting from our habitual patterns without consciousness, i.e., when we have a "knee-jerk" reaction. Mindfulness helps us to become more aware of our patterns and provides the pause needed to make a different choice. With daily practice, we become less reactive, more present, and less likely to operate on automatic pilot.

When we have equanimity, we have more patience and serenity, as well as fewer attachments. We may still have preferences, but we can "go with the flow" and not stress about how things will shake out. We may have big hopes and dreams, yet we're able to accept any possible outcome.

Some have misunderstood equanimity to be apathy, inactivity, or denial. When we have equanimity, we still stand up for what we believe in and take action, but we are more likely to take *wise* action since we are operating from a calm and balanced state of mind rather than from reactivity. When we are grounded in equanimity, we communicate our point of view with more respect, reasoning, and effectiveness.

Another myth is that having equanimity means that there is a lack of emotion. Again, if we feel numb, this is not equanimity. Mindfulness softens our attachments to how we think life "should" unfold. And when we don't have these attachments, we can be *more* present and engaged at any given moment.

Let's use the example of a wedding day to illustrate this point. If the bride is equanimous, she will experience incredible happiness during the event, but not crave the bliss once the wedding is over. Knowing that the day will end inspires her to be even more present, alive, and generous with her guests. And, let's say that it rains for part of the wedding ceremony. If the groom is equanimous, he might feel slightly annoyed as the raindrops fall, but he can quickly shift back to feeling at ease since he knows the rain will eventually pass. Even though there are high expectations on their wedding day, this equanimous couple neither cling to the good nor push away the bad—they are willing to let the day unfold just as it is.

Acceptance is the Key

We develop the mental and emotional stability of equanimity through the power of acceptance. When we let go of resistance to our circumstances and fully accept the way things are, we experience the ease and strength of equanimity.[1]

One way to cultivate equanimity informally is by repeating the following phrases throughout the day:

- Things are as they are; may I accept things just as they are.
- He is who he is; may I accept him just as he is.
- She is who she is; may I accept her just as she is.
- I am who I am; may I accept myself just as I am.

The reason why the word "may" is included in these phrases is because oftentimes our circumstances are hard to accept. So, as an act of self-compassion, we can say, "*may* I accept this circumstance." Including the word "may" makes the statement more accessible when the circumstance is too difficult to accept right away.

After weeks of repeating this phrase, we can possibly get to a place where we can accept the circumstance outright, take out the word "may", and say to ourselves, *Things are as they are, I accept things just as they are.*

We can also repeat these phrases as a formal practice, such as during our morning meditation. This way, we accumulate a reserve of ease and strength that we can tap into later in the day when a tough moment arises.

The Eight Worldly Winds

Life is always going to present an array of ups and downs, good and bad, positive and negative. We can try our best to manage our circumstances, but, as I learned the hard way with my cancer diagnosis, we ultimately don't have control over what happens in life.

The Buddhist concept of the Eight Worldly Winds[2] presents four pairs of opposites that continually appear in life:

- Wherever there is praise, there will be blame.
- Wherever there is success, there will be failure.
- Wherever there is pleasure, there will be pain.
- Wherever there is fame, there will be disgrace.

As humans, we are always compulsively grasping for the positive of the pair and pushing away the negative. Most of our lives, we are tied to the currents of these back-and-forth energies, playing the victim of our circumstances.

We begin to awaken when we realize that these winds are inevitable. Although we don't have control over some of our circumstances in life, we can change how we relate to them by cultivating a nonreactive mind. Rather than constantly trying to manage these winds, we can spend all of that energy developing an equanimous mindset that can *be* with the ups and downs of life with grace.

The allegory of the Buddha becoming enlightened under the Bodhi tree is the most renowned example of the power of equanimity. Buddha experienced enlightenment the moment he neither clung to nor pushed away any thought, emotion, or experience. In that moment of pure equanimity, he became entirely available for the changing stream of life—he became fully awake.

The Heart Qualities

In Buddhism, equanimity is one of the four *Brahmaviharas*, or heart qualities—the other three are joy, loving-kindness, and compassion. These four qualities are also known as the Four Immeasurable Minds because when we practice them, they grow so large within us that they can expand indefinitely. We become happier, and everyone around us also becomes happier.[3]

Each of the four qualities contains the other; therefore, equanimity is also an expression of joy, loving-kindness, and compassion. Equanimity dissolves thoughts of craving and aversion, creating the space for joy, loving-kindness, and compassion to grow.

With equanimity, we create the fertile soil for the heart qualities to blossom. If we get upset about "every little thing," we miss out on the joy that is always available within us. Equanimity allows us to roll with the punches and fully experience the heart qualities, regardless of the challenges happening in our lives.

Equanimity and Joy

To activate the joy within, we must understand what the essence of joy actually is. The first step is to distinguish between the experiences of hope, joy, and happiness. Hope is the belief that something good is going to happen. Joy is knowing that goodness is already here. Happiness is the visceral experience of having the goal achieved.

To illustrate this point, let's say we are walking through a hot desert and we're incredibly thirsty, we would hope that a stream was nearby. Joy would be experienced when we actually see the stream in the distance—there is an added level of excitement and relief since we know that cool water is coming soon. Upon drinking the water, our thirst is quenched, and we are filled with happiness.

The difference between hope and joy is the level of conviction. To be hopeful is to believe that a stream is nearby, yet there is still a tinge of doubt. Joy is experienced by having a deeper knowing that there will *always* be a stream when we need one, resulting in a consistent feeling of ease—therefore, shifting from hope to joy requires a level of faith. We live in joy when we believe that the potential for happiness exists in every moment, even if we haven't attained our goal yet.

Equanimity helps us to shift from hope to joy in that it softens our attachments to the outcome of our goals. This practice also cultivates non-reactivity and trust regarding how our lives are unfolding.

We can think of these three mental states as a pathway, starting with hope, then joy, and then ultimately happiness:

Hope (optimism) –> Joy (excitement and ease) –> Happiness (satisfaction/goal attained)

When we lose hope, however, we fall off of this path altogether, and into a state of despair. Whenever I felt despair during my year with cancer, I remembered the power of staying hopeful and the importance of getting back onto this path to joy and happiness. For my mental wellbeing, I was committed to staying optimistic and hopeful.

It seems that everyone is trying to be happy, but the emotion of happiness comes and goes since it is contingent on circumstances. But hope and joy can be constant states of mind. Rather than seek happiness (which is a moving target), we can set a daily intention to have a joyful mindset. So, when circumstances change and happiness is no longer present, we can continue to experience joy in our lives.

If a joyful mindset seems out of reach, the book *Hardwiring Happiness,* by neuropsychologist Rick Hanson, offers practical tools to rewire the brain. Hanson says that a positive mindset can be cultivated by savoring good experiences in our lives for at least five to ten seconds.

So, rather than constantly checking our phones when we are taking a sunset walk on the beach, we can put our phones away and take the time to appreciate the colors on the water. During such positive experiences, Hanson instructs us to say to ourselves, "Stay with this," along with taking deep breaths, which activate the calming parasympathetic nervous system. We can also express appreciation by saying, "Thank you for this beautiful sunset." This establishes mental patterns of gratitude. With repetition of these practices, we can create a lasting mindset of joy.

Another way to cultivate joy is to not compare ourselves with others, which can be challenging as we scroll through our social media feeds. Former president Theodore Roosevelt is quoted as saying, "Comparison is the thief of joy." Buddhist philosophy offers the concept of sympathetic joy, which is the feeling of rejoicing in someone else's good fortune. When we hear about a friend getting a job promotion, we can be happy and inspired by their accomplishment rather than feeling jealous or inadequate.

Equanimity practice neutralizes feelings of envy or resentment so that our sympathetic joy is sincere. Dropping into the wisdom that we are all connected at the soul level makes sympathetic joy more authentic since we acknowledge that our friend's happiness is also our own.

Equanimity and Loving-Kindness

The second heart quality is loving-kindness, or simply kindness. Loving-kindness is engaging in kind action toward another person and offering well wishes for their happiness.

Loving-kindness and equanimity are good compliments for each other as daily practices. Loving-kindness connects us to our hearts and brings love and warmth to equanimity. Equanimity brings balance and wisdom to loving-kindness so that we are not overly loving toward those who may take advantage of our kindness. Setting respectful boundaries is a form of having equanimity. Particularly for caregivers, equanimity practice can help prevent us from giving too much and burning out.

Loving-kindness is a natural quality of the heart and is quite easy to cultivate. All we need to do is think about someone we care about and wish them well. It can be a person or an animal that we love.

To do the Loving-Kindness practice, close your eyes, imagine a loved one sitting in front of you and offer them these well-wishes:

- May you be happy.
- May you be peaceful.
- May you be safe and protected.
- May you be healthy in body and mind.

We can rewrite and personalize the phrases. Once we've offered loving-kindness to our loved ones, we have warmed our hearts, enabling us to continue to send these well-wishes to friends, acquaintances, and even to ourselves.

If our hearts are warm enough, perhaps we can send loving-kindness to people we despise. If we are not able to authentically say these phrases toward our enemies quite yet, we can start with the equanimity phrase—*They are who they are, may I accept them just as they are*—and then notice how we feel.

Equanimity helps us to offer loving-kindness in a more genuine way. It clears our agendas, attachments, and resentments, which creates the space for pure loving-kindness to be expressed. Repeating the loving-kindness phrases throughout the day can be a simple way to enhance the level of happiness we feel in our lives.

Equanimity and Compassion

Compassion is different from loving-kindness in that it wishes another person to be free from their suffering. Compassion contains the qualities of both care and strength. When we show compassion for another, we are typically in action motivated by our sincere desire to help relieve their suffering.

This formula identifies the qualities of compassion and shows the role of equanimity:

Empathy (caring) + Equanimity (strength) = Compassion (the desire to alleviate suffering)

To illustrate the concept, let's say three people witness a car accident—an empathic person, an equanimous person, and a compassionate person. The empath may get too overwhelmed with distress to be able to take action. The equanimous person may take action but without the qualities of care and kindness that may be required. The compassionate person, however, can drop into their heart and care deeply for the victims while taking the best course of action to relieve their suffering.

We can use the formula (Empathy + Equanimity = Compassion) to cultivate more compassion within ourselves. On any given day, we can assess whether we need to develop more empathy or equanimity. Some of us may be excessively equanimous and feel disconnected in our relationships. Rather than judge ourselves as cold or uncaring, we can cultivate empathy with loving-kindness practice and become a more compassionate version of ourselves.

To have empathy means to feel what another person is feeling. The way empathy occurs is when we see another person's face, our mirror neurons mimic what we see so that we feel what the other person is feeling. For example, when someone smiles at us, we instinctively smile back, and we both experience what it is to smile.

In his book *Emotional Intelligence,* researcher Daniel Goleman shows that mindfulness improves our ability to be empathic. Specifically, loving-kindness phrases activate the insula, the part of the brain that contains a high concentration of mirror neurons. Therefore, when we say loving-kindness phrases on our meditation cushion, we become more empathic out in the world.

Many of us are highly empathic and have spent much of our lives soaking in chaotic energies from the environment and judging ourselves for being "too sensitive."

Since I've discovered the equanimity practice, however, I no longer need to squelch my sensitivity or "toughen up." Instead, I cultivate strength and poise through equanimity practice and alchemize my empathy into compassion.

By adding equanimity to our caring, empathic nature, we build the composure of the compassionate mind. Rather than our reactivity taking over when challenges arise, we are able to handle challenges with both kindness and with strength.

Cultivating the Equanimous Mind

In his book *Mindsight*, clinical professor of psychiatry Dan Siegel coined the term "Window of Tolerance" to describe the amount of stimuli a person can handle with resilience.

Everyone's window of tolerance is different. Those with a wider window may experience greater equanimity and be able to handle intense situations with grace. Those who have a narrow window may feel as if their emotions are intense and hard to manage.

On any given day, challenging events occur that bring our nervous system to the upper or lower edges of our window. At the upper edge is fear or anger, and the lower edge is sadness.

A Regulated Nervous System

Balanced — Window of Tolerance is Wide

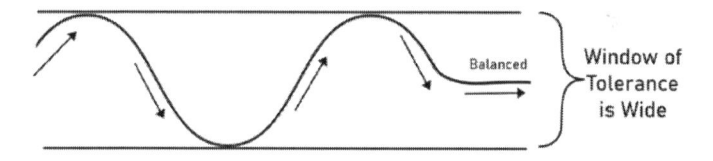

A Dysregulated Nervous System

Traumatic Event

Stuck on "On" (chronic anxiety)

Stuck on "Off" (chronic depression)

Window of Tolerance is Narrow

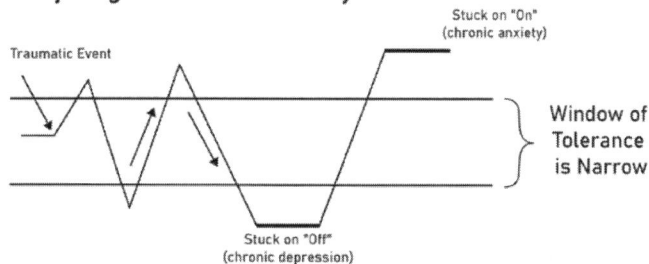

With a regulated nervous system (which has a wide window of tolerance), we are able to roll with the ups and downs of life, use coping strategies to balance our nervous system, and stay within our window.

With a dysregulated nervous system (which has a narrow window of tolerance), the same stimuli can occur, but we can become overwhelmed or shut down and unable to bounce back into equilibrium. Without emotional coping strategies, we can get "stuck" either above the window (leading to chronic anxiety or anger) or below the window (leading to chronic depression).

Siegel's research shows that traumatic experiences (such as receiving a cancer diagnosis) can narrow the window of tolerance. This means that we have a reduced capacity to handle challenges in life and a greater tendency to become overwhelmed or shut down.

How to Expand the Window of Tolerance

It's important to remember that there is nothing wrong with being out of our window of tolerance. Getting "stuck" either in anxiety, hostility, or depression from time to time is a natural part of the human experience. Having regular practices in mindfulness and equanimity help us to become "unstuck" from these emotional states and develop emotional resilience.

Here are three practical ways to widen our window of tolerance:

1. Mindfulness: Siegel's research shows that practicing mindfulness not only keeps our nervous system in balance, it expands our window of tolerance. When we are triggered, mindfulness brings us back into our window by activating the prefrontal cortex, which regulates the nervous system. Specifically, the prefrontal cortex calms the amygdala by releasing the amino acid GABA. Mindfulness also soothes the limbic system, which slows the breathing and heart rate after an emotionally triggering experience. Also, the prefrontal cortex can reframe traumatic memories with wisdom, therefore regulating the hippocampus (the brain's storehouse of memories).[4]

2. Safety: People who have experienced trauma may believe the world is unsafe and operate from a narrow window of tolerance. Therefore, creating an environment where we feel safe and supported can help us to stay in our window and maintain a regulated nervous system.[5]

3. Grounding or Stimulating Activities: When we notice that our nervous system has become overwhelmed or shut down, we can do specific activities to bring ourselves back into balance. When we are angry or anxious, lying under a weighted blanket, walking barefoot on the grass, or taking deep breaths while extending the exhale are activities that can ground us and bring us back into our window. When we are depressed, we can do stimulating activities such as exercising, dancing to upbeat music, or taking deep breaths while elongating the inhale.

With daily mindfulness practice, we widen our window of tolerance little by little, and cultivate higher levels of emotional resilience. By consciously choosing to spend time in environments that feel safe, along with consciously doing activities that bring our nervous system back into balance, we develop a greater ability to handle challenges with grace.

Sharon Brock, M.S.

The Equanimity Practice Meditation

Listen to the meditation online at:
www.meditationforbreastcancer.com

Let's begin by gently closing the eyes or lowering your gaze to the floor. Bringing both feet flat on the ground, sitting up tall while relaxing the shoulders and the arms, allowing your hands to lay comfortably on your lap. Taking a few deep breaths in and out of the nose, allowing the body to soften and become still.

I'd like you to bring to mind a situation where you *had* equanimity. It doesn't have to be a big deal, just a hard situation from the past week that you handled with a balanced mind. Where did it take place? Who else was there? How did it feel when you were equanimous? Bring your attention into your body, and tap into that feeling of equanimity. Allow yourself to experience the qualities of feeling grounded, spacious, and calm. Where do you feel equanimity in your body? Getting to know what equanimity feels like in the body.

Now bring to mind a situation that has been triggering for you, and you feel like you *don't* have equanimity. Maybe there's a person in your life that you're having a hard time with. Or a circumstance you're dealing with and having a hard time accepting. You have resistance—you're wishing the circumstance was different, or you're wishing that this other person was different.

Notice how you feel inside the body when you think about this situation. Perhaps there is contraction, pressure or tension in the body. There is no right or wrong, just notice—how do you feel when you think about this challenging circumstance?

Now we will repeat the equanimity phrases, and notice if

anything changes in the way that you feel. Choose the phrase that best fits your circumstance:

Things are as they are; may I accept things just as they are.
He is who he is; may I accept him just as he is.
She is who she is; may I accept her just as she is.
I am as I am; may I accept myself just as I am.

Gently and lovingly repeat your chosen phrase over and over again in your mind. Noticing any changes in your mood or sensations in the body as you repeat these words:

Things are as they are; may I accept things just as they are.

Continue to breathe and repeat the equanimity phrase. Noticing what is happening in your body and mind. If there are no changes, that is also okay. We aren't forcing anything. To be mindful is to simply notice whatever is here in the present moment with acceptance, openness, and curiosity.

Continue repeating your chosen phrase.

If an emotion arises during the practice, such as anger, anxiety or sadness, there is no problem—we can allow the emotion to be here and simply bring mindfulness to it. We can label the emotion, such as, "anger is here," or "sadness is rising." We can bring our hands to our hearts and embrace this emotion, and lovingly say to ourselves, *Along with holding this difficult circumstance with kindness, may I also hold this emotion with kindness.*

Continue repeating your chosen phrase. *Things are as they are; may I accept things just as they are.*

Every time you repeat the phrase you are cultivating equanimity. You are rewiring your brain to be more accepting, less reactive, and you're expanding your ability to handle life's hardships with grace.

Now shift your attention to the first scenario where you *did* feel equanimity, filling up your body with the qualities of strength and grace, and then offering those qualities to the second, more challenging circumstance. Since you've demonstrated your ability to be equanimous in the first scenario, imagine yourself handling the second circumstance with a balanced, nonreactive mind. Continuing to breathe. Imagining yourself handling your challenging circumstance with ease, strength, and grace.

If you're not feeling equanimity, that's also perfectly okay. Just bring acceptance and mindfulness to whatever is here. If you are feeling equanimity, take a few deep breaths and allow this essence of ease and strength to spread throughout your body. Feeling the essence of strength filling up your legs and into your abdomen. Feeling the light of grace filling your chest and heart, up your neck, to your face, and out the crown of your head. Your entire body is emanating ease, strength, and grace. Take a deep breath in, bathing in the beautiful light of equanimity.

As we begin to bring our meditation to a close, feeling your feet on the ground, feeling your seat on the chair or cushion, feeling your hands on your lap. Taking in a deep breath, filling up the abdomen, and exhaling out your mouth. And when you're ready, gently blink open your eyes.

Part 6
Putting LOVEE Altogether

Chapter 16
After Cancer, Challenges Still Arise

*"In the depth of winter, I finally learned that
there was in me an invincible summer."*
Albert Camus, philosopher

The Birthday Party

After a few weeks of recovery from surgery, I started to plan my birthday party. I rarely threw birthday parties for myself, but I was not holding back for this one. I had *earned* this birthday. I was turning 45, and I had more birthdays in my future, which was cause for a huge celebration. I invited more than 100 people, decorated my backyard with twinkly lights, and set up a large speaker to blast my favorite dance music. It was time to celebrate life!

On the morning of the party, I looked in the mirror and noticed that my hair was still deranged from chemo. It had fallen out in a quasi mohawk pattern—more hair on top and less on the sides. Not the cool type of mohawk worn by trendsetters, but more like mohawk meets train wreck. In a moment of self-pity, I thought, *I didn't choose the mohawk, the mohawk chose me.*

I recalled one of my favorite Eckhart Tolle quotes, "Whatever the present moment contains, accept it as if you had chosen it. Always work with it, not against it."

I was tired of cancer dictating what my life looked like, or what *I* looked like, so I took Eckhart's advice and I thought, *I'm going to decide how my hair looks tonight at my birthday party. I am* choosing *the damn mohawk!*

I picked up the phone and called my friend Liz who was a hairdresser at a trendy salon on Melrose Avenue.

"Hey Sharon, happy birthday!" Liz said as she answered the phone. "I'm excited about the party tonight."

"Hey Liz," I said. "I'm so glad you're coming! Would you mind coming over early? My hair has fallen out in all sorts of weird ways. And, I'd love for you to … give me a mohawk?" I thought to myself, *I can't believe I just said those words out loud.*

"Of course! I've been waiting all my life for you to say that," she said with a laugh. I typically wore a conservative bob haircut, so Liz was delighted for me to try something edgy. "I'll be right over."

Liz arrived, and we set up a chair in the living room. She used clippers to buzz the sides evenly. She shaped the center section of my hair and lifted it with styling products for a sophisticated mohawk look. I looked in the mirror and cringed, still figuring out if I liked it or not.

"What a badass," Liz said with a smile. "Do you want racing stripes?"

"Do I want *what*?" I asked. Liz showed me a photograph of a woman with a mohawk with two lines forming an "X" buzzed onto her scalp.

"Hell yeah, I do!" I said, shifting my fear into excitement. Liz smiled and continued her artistry. "Since I'm making lemonade out of lemons," I said, "I might as well make lemonade margaritas!"

As Liz was finishing, my other friend Ivy came over to do my makeup. I felt pampered as Ivy brushed power across my face, colored my eyelids with shimmery shadow, and put glitter on my cheekbones. Since I had lost most of my eye-lashes from chemo, it was especially sweet when she applied false lashes. It was the first time I'd felt pretty in a very long time.

"You look beautiful," Ivy said with a teary smile. "And, now, I have a surprise for you. This will make your outfit complete." Ivy offered me hand-sewn butterfly wings for me to wear as a cape. "These are in honor of your amazing metamorphosis," she said.

"Wow, these are gorgeous!" I exclaimed. "That is so sweet of you. Thank you so much!"

I quickly changed into a long black dress so that the yellow and orange colors of the monarch butterfly wings would pop. I had officially evolved

The LOVEE Method

out of my chrysalis, and it was time for this butterfly to spread her wings and fly!

With my friend Ivy at my birthday party.

As more friends arrived, we opened the bar and cranked up the music. My heart was filled with happiness to see so many friends I loved altogether in one place. We ate, drank, laughed, and danced around a blazing fire pit in my backyard.

I began to hear people singing "Happy Birthday" and I turned around to see my friend, Maya, carrying a huge tiramisu cake covered in candles. Everyone stopped their conversations and started to join the happy birthday song. Before blowing out the candles, I took a moment to look around at my cherished friends who were circling around me. I felt held in a container of so much friendship, love, and support.

Filled with gratitude, I closed my eyes and made three wishes. I wished that everyone at the party would have excellent health in their lives. I wished that every woman going through breast cancer felt as loved and supported as I did at that moment. Thirdly, I wished for a cancer-free world. I blew out the candles, and everyone cheered!

After finishing my piece of tiramisu, Alyssa came up to me and said, "Can you come inside real quick? I have a birthday present for you."

"Sure, of course," I said. We walked into the living room and sat down on the sofa. Alyssa handed me a birthday card.

"Aww, thank you," I said. "You didn't have to get me a card."

"Well, there's a bigger gift inside," she said. That piqued my interest and I opened the card with excitement. The card read:

> Happy Birthday, Sharon!
> Cancer shouldn't stand in the way of your dreams. I'd like to pay for your trip to Spain so that you can live your dream of walking the Camino. You deserve it!
> Love,
> Alyssa

My eyes popped open. "What?" I said. "Oh no, Alyssa, that's too much."

"It's okay," she said. "It was such a wonderful trip for me, and I want you to have that experience."

"But I couldn't accept that money from you," I said. "It's too much."

"Don't worry, I have the money," she said. "It would mean a lot to me if you accepted it and lived your dream of taking this trip. It wasn't fair that cancer took the money that you saved for this trip. I want to right that wrong."

"Wow, well, thank you so much," I said with teary eyes. "I can't believe how generous you are."

"Honestly, you've been through so much," she said. "Thank *you* for being such an inspiration for all of us. You deserve to go and live this dream."

"Okay, well … thank you!" I said and hugged her. She gave me a big smile and then returned to the party.

I walked into my bedroom to take a breath and process this offering. I was incredibly touched—no one had ever given me such a generous gift. Although I knew Alyssa didn't want anything in return, I wondered how I would repay her. In any case, I promised myself that I would pay this gift forward in some way.

People Come into Our Lives for a Reason, a Season, or a Lifetime

The next day, I was feeling grateful for the support of my friends throughout this challenging time and how lovely it was for us all to be together to celebrate the end of the journey.

I was also excited that my vacation to Spain was actually going to happen. Although my body wouldn't be ready for this physical feat for several months, trekking 100 miles would be the next milestone for me to achieve—the Camino would be my victory lap!

That night, I had a date with Will. Since he couldn't attend my birthday party due to work obligations, he made it up to me by getting reservations at the Magic Castle, an exclusive dinner-and-magic show in Hollywood. While putting on my fanciest cocktail dress and heels, I was brimming with excitement for an enchanting night of love and laughter with my sweetheart.

I heard Will's car park in the driveway. When the doorbell rang, I spritzed one last burst of hair spray to keep my mohawk upright, then opened the door.

"Ta-daaa!" I said, with jazz hands on either side of my head. "Do you like it?" I asked. I turned my head sideways to showcase the mohawk profile in all of its glory.

"Whoa!" he said. "I love it. It looks great!"

"Have you ever gone out with a woman with a mohawk before?" I asked, walking to his car.

"I can't say that I have," he said with a laugh. "And since we'll be in Hollywood, your mohawk will fit right in."

As we approached the Magic Castle, I admired the Victorian mansion sitting magnificently on top of a hill. Upon entering the castle, I was struck by the tall ceilings with ornate crown molding, the red velvet walls adorned with alluring oil portraits, and dark-wood sculptures of mythical creatures. With magic around every corner, Will and I had dropped into a land of enchantment for the night.

After dinner, we walked down a winding staircase and explored a labyrinth of hidden rooms where magicians showcased their craft. After a few awe-inspiring magic shows, we discovered an intimate bar to share the last drink of the night.

"Happy birthday, Sharon!" Will said, raising a glass of red wine.

"Thank you, sweetheart," I said, and clinked his glass.

"Isn't this place amazing?" he asked.

"Yes, I love it. This is the perfect birthday present," I said, gushing. "Thank you, love."

"I'm so glad you like it," he said, putting his arm around my shoulders.

I took a sip of wine, then said, "So, I looked at flights today."

"To where?" he asked, sitting back in his chair.

"To Spain," I said. "Remember when I was planning to walk the Camino before all of this happened? Well, that trip is back on. I'm going in a few months, after I get my strength back."

"That's great!" he said. "I'm so happy to hear that."

"Yeah, I'm really excited," I said. "So … do you still want to go with me?"

"Oh, right," he said. "Umm, I'm not sure. Things have gotten really hard with my ex-wife. I'm going through a rough patch right now."

"Oh?" I asked, feeling both surprised and uncomfortable. Suddenly, the magic of the night was starting to fade. "Is everything okay?"

"Yeah, I'm alright," he said. "We've been working on our house, getting ready to sell it, so it's been hard to be around each other so much."

"Right," I said. A rush of jealousy swept through me. "Is there a chance that you two will get back together?"

"Oh, no," he said. "That definitely won't happen."

"Oh, okay," I said, relieved. We both picked up our wine glasses. He took a sip, and I took a gulp. Maybe it was the magic, maybe it was the wine, but I decided to take a risk and tell him how I really felt about him.

"So … since it's my birthday," I said, "I want to tell you something."

"Of course," he said, smiling. "What's up?"

"It's really vulnerable, but I just have to tell you," I said, sheepishly.

"Oh?" he asked. "What is it?"

"Well … I'm in love with you," I said. "All I want for my birthday … is you. To be in partnership with you. I just want to love you up."

There was a long pause. He looked down and I scanned his face for clues. Even though we were surrounded by laughter and revelry, we sat there silent, like the statues hovering in the corners.

To fill the awkward silence, I said, "Well, I just thought you should know."

He looked up at me and said, "You mean a lot to me, Sharon. I really care about you, and I love spending time with you."

"Okay, I got it," I said, feeling the rejection and finishing my wine.

"I'm going through a lot of pain with my ex right now. I'm not ready for another serious relationship," he said. "I don't know if I'll ever be ready. It's just too painful when it ends."

"Okay, right," I said. I wanted to tell him that it would be different with me; that I would love him forever and never hurt him. But I also knew it was important to respect where he was coming from and give him the space he needed.

"I'm going to go to the restroom," I said. "I'll be right back."

As I walked along the hallway where we came in, the beautiful mansion turned into a haunted house in my mind—the statues of mythical creatures turned into gargoyles, and the oil portraits transformed into ghostly paintings. The night had turned from magic to macabre, and the enchantment of the evening transmuted into a darkness that shrouded my being.

In the restroom, I began to tear up. I was hurt, frustrated, and disappointed. I tried to understand his point of view and not take the conversation personally. Thinking back on our time together, it was clear that he was not available for partnership. The signs were there, but I didn't want to see them. Although I was the one who had major surgery a few weeks ago, he was the one who had a lot more healing to do.

Having cancer, I learned that I was not in control of my circumstances. I now had to apply this same lesson to my love life. I had to accept where Will was emotionally, and let go.

As an act of self-love, it was time to stop dating him since we wanted different things. During cancer treatment, I had made a commitment to myself to always make the most self-loving choice, and I wasn't going to stop now. In this case, although it was painful, that choice was to walk away.

By the time I returned to the table, Will had paid the check and was getting ready to leave. On the drive back to my house, we held hands but didn't say a word. In my mind, I thought about *his* journey and the pain he must have been going through during the time we were together. I looked at him with eyes of compassion and gratitude. Sadness also welled up in my heart since I knew the conversation we were about to have.

When we arrived at my house, Will parked the car in my driveway and took off his seatbelt.

"Maybe you shouldn't come in," I said, staying seated.

"Oh, well, I still want to see you, Sharon," he said. "It doesn't have to end between us."

"I've got to unhook from you, Will," I said. "If we want different things, then I need to move on. If we keep seeing each other casually, it would be too hard on me."

"Okay," he said. "I guess so." Tears started to well up in his eyes.

"Seems like this was the hardest year in *both* of our lives," I said. "We both went through a metamorphosis."

"Yeah," he said. "Thanks for putting your cocoon next to mine."

"Aww," I said with a teary smile. "Thank you for being an angel in my life; you got me through a really hard time."

The LOVEE Method

"You really helped me, too, Sharon," he said. "We were angels for each other."

I leaned over and kissed him, knowing it would be the last.

"Bye, Will," I said. "Take care of yourself."

"You, too," he said. I got out of the car and walked to my doorstep. We waved good-bye to each other, and I watched him drive away.

I stumbled into my room and laid down on my bed. The moment my head hit the pillow, I fell apart. I beat my fists on my bed, crying in pain. My emotion shifted from sadness to anger. *This isn't fair! I just went through cancer, and now I have to deal with* this?

Then came the grief. The thought of Will no longer in my life—the daily texts, the sweet words, the romantic dinners—caused my heart to break. Tears of grief and sorrow came pouring out.

After about twenty minutes of crying, I remembered.

Wait, I know what to do.

I took a deep breath, got out of bed, and sat down on my meditation pillow, and mentally went through the steps of the LOVEE Method:

Label:
Grief is here.

Observe:
I'm observing grief in my body; I feel it in my chest, my heart is pounding. I'm not judging it; I don't need to get over it right away; It can be here as long as it needs to be.

Value:
I'm not alone—people go through heartbreak every day. Loss is a natural part of life, and it's natural to feel grief when we feel loss. Even though this is hard, I value this experience. The amount of grief I feel is equivalent to the amount of love I feel for him. Feeling this grief means that I am alive, and I value this precious life.

I brought my hands to my heart and cradled the grief energy as if it were a small child.

Embrace:
I see you, little one. I hear you. I know you're sad. It's okay to be sad. I'm here for you. I'm listening. What do you need, sweetheart? ... Love? Safety? I love you. I will always love you. And I'll always be here for you. You are safe with me.

Equanimity:
I accept that Will is not available emotionally for partnership. He is who he is; may I accept him just as he is. Things are as they are; may I accept things just as they are.

I felt better. The grief was still there, but my nervous system relaxed and became balanced. Of course, I was disappointed and wished things were different, but I also felt grateful for Will. During this deeply vulnerable time, he offered me kindness, laughter and support—all things that were incredibly healing. But I also knew that it was time to turn the page and start a new chapter in my life.

Chapter 17
The LOVEE Method—Build Emotional Resilience

*"I am no longer afraid of storms, for I am
learning how to sail my ship."*
Louisa May Alcott, author

Learning to Suffer "Well"

It seemed that life carried on after cancer. Just because I was cancer-free, that didn't mean life was going to be sunshine and rainbows moving forward. Hard times were here again, but I was no longer afraid because I now had the LOVEE Method in my emotional resilience toolbox.

In his book *Reconciliation*, Thich Nhat Hanh says, "Knowing how to suffer 'well' is essential to realizing true happiness." Although I was still recovering emotionally, the LOVEE Method enabled me to suffer "well" since this practice continually transformed my grief into loving awareness.

Since I applied the LOVEE Method to the breakup with Will, this tool had proven its value beyond my health crisis. It was clear that regular practice of the LOVEE Method was essential for my happiness in *all* areas of my life—the more I practiced, the more I expanded my loving awareness. So rather than seeing life's challenges as setbacks, I now saw them as opportunities to grow.

Empowerment in Your Pocket

Emotional resilience is developed with regular practice of mindfulness, self-compassion, and equanimity—and the LOVEE Method includes all three of these components. With the mindfulness practices of "L" and "O", we label emotions as they arise, and observe them in the body rather than judge or push them away. During the self-compassion practices of "V" and "E", we value our emotions as natural aspects of being human, and embrace them with love and compassion. With the equanimity practice, "E", we bring our nervous system back into balance and cultivate a nonreactive mind through the power of acceptance and releasing resistance to our circumstances.

Since the LOVEE Method contains all three elements of mindfulness, self-compassion and equanimity, it is a comprehensive tool that cultivates emotional resilience, allowing us to handle the inevitable hardships of life with grace.

We can practice each letter separately or string them together as a single tool to be used whenever a challenging emotion arises. The LOVEE Method creates a safe container in which the painful emotion can rise, peak, and fade away. Therefore, it provides a healthy way to process and integrate our emotions.

When we get emotionally triggered, rather than suppress or react to the emotion, we can confidently move through the steps of the LOVEE Method. Here's a simple rundown of each practice to demonstrate how they work altogether:

Step 1: "L" is for Label—Label the Emotion

When an intense emotion arises, find a private place to practice, take a few deep breaths, and then label the emotion, such as, "anger is rising." When we label the emotion, we create a space between ourselves and the emotion, called the "mindful gap." It's important not to identify with the emotion, so rather than say, "*I* am angry," we can say, "anger is rising." In this step, we acknowledge the anger for what it actually is—an energy in motion. Emotions are not personal to us; they are energies of varying frequencies that rise and fall in our experience throughout the day.

Step 2: "O" is for Observe—Observe the Emotion

We have two minds: the thinking mind (the voice in our head) and the observing mind (the awareness that *observes* the thinking mind). In mindfulness meditation, we take the point of view of the observing mind.

After the Label practice, the next step is to pinpoint the location of the emotion in the body and observe it without trying to change it. We often criticize ourselves for becoming angry, anxious, or depressed. But rather than judgment, we can bring a sense of curiosity to the sensation of the emotion and simply observe it as it escalates in intensity and then eventually fades away. Rather than bottling up our emotions, the Observe practice lets them "run their course" so that the energy is processed and released in a healthy way.

Step 3: "V" is for Value—Value the Emotion

Rather than resist our challenging emotions, we can value them. Since challenging emotions are shared among all humans, they connect us to each other. When we are upset, we tend to shut down and isolate ourselves, but during the Value practice, we remember that we are not alone in feeling this way and others would feel the same way in this circumstance. These emotions are natural to the human condition, and there is nothing "wrong" with having them. It is comforting to know that we are all on this human journey, learning, growing, and evolving together.

Also, we can value our emotion because it may have something to tell us. If you're feeling anxiety, for example, this may be revealing that you're feeling unsafe and it's time to create safety in your environment. If you're feeling anger, perhaps you need to set some boundaries. If you're feeling sadness, it's either time to connect with others or let something go.

Lastly, these challenging emotions provide contrast. It is *because* we feel anxiety that we don't take it for granted when we feel ease. It is *because* of the hard times that we don't take it for granted when things are going well. Happiness doesn't exist without sadness, so we can value these two emotions equally. Valuing our challenging emotions means that we are valuing the full spectrum of the human experience, and what it is to be a whole human being. With the Value practice, we cultivate appreciation for the fact that we are alive and we *get* to experience these emotions. With this practice, we become more grateful for our lives and recognize the preciousness of life itself.

Step 4: "E" is for Embrace—Embrace the Emotion

In this step, we offer love and compassion for the emotion itself. Rather than resisting or judging the emotion, we bring our hands to our hearts and embrace it as if it were a small child. Like a loving parent, we offer the emotion kind words, such as: *I love you. I see you. I hear you. What do you need?*

Then, we listen carefully. If the emotion is anger, it may need respect. If it is anxiety, it may need safety. If it is depression, it may need connection. From a place of deep compassion, we can comfort the emotion by saying such phrases: *I respect you. I'll keep you safe. I care about you and I'll always be here for you.*

Rather than seeking to get our emotional needs met from others, this practice allows us to meet our own needs to feel whole and complete within ourselves. Therefore, this self-compassion practice promotes independence, empowerment, and self-confidence.

Step 5: "E" is for Equanimity—Accept the Situation

Once the emotion has been soothed and processed with the L-O-V-E steps, we bring our attention back to the original triggering circumstance. This last step cultivates equanimity, or a nonreactive mind. By mentally repeating the equanimity phrase, *Things are as they are; may I accept things just as they are*, we release resistance to the situation and generate feelings of acceptance, strength, and ease. With equanimity, we bring our nervous system back into balance allowing us to respond to the circumstance from a place of reasoning and wisdom rather than a place of upset.

The LOVEE Method Shortcut

If we don't have enough time to stop and practice the full LOVEE Method, we can try this shortcut: *Observe it. Love it.* We can say this phrase throughout the day to remind ourselves to observe our thoughts and emotions as they rise and fall, as well as offer them compassion.

Applying The LOVEE Method to Different Areas of Life

At Work

During the workday, there are countless challenges that we must handle with composure. The LOVEE Method can help calm our nerves before giving a big presentation, focus our minds while on a tight deadline, and soothe our emotions when working with challenging co-workers. When we address and meet our own emotional needs, we increase our bandwidth for higher productivity and creativity.

Since maintaining professionalism at work is paramount, the LOVEE Method can help balance our intense emotions on the spot. If we get anxious about our lengthy to-do list or angry with an unappreciative boss, we can take a break and use the LOVEE Method to attain emotional resilience and bring our nervous system back into balance.

The LOVEE Method also enhances leadership in that it increases self-awareness, confidence, and emotional intelligence. The Label practice, in particular, increases emotional intelligence by honing the skill of identifying emotions within ourselves and others. When managers have a higher emotional intelligence, they are more effective leaders because they are able to identify their employee's strengths and create opportunities for them to thrive.

Parenting

Working with children requires an incredible amount of patience and when we lose our temper, we often feel guilty. Without mindfulness, the unconscious cycle of lashing out and then feeling guilt continues without a clear end in sight. With the LOVEE Method, we can catch ourselves when we get to our wit's end and use the practice to bring us back to center, so that we may *respond* to our children, rather than *react*.

It's also important to remember that emotions are "energies in motion" and have a life-cycle of only 90 seconds. Therefore, when a child is having a tantrum, rather than react, parents can allow the emotion in their child to run its course and dissolve on its own. Parents can remain equanimous during the tantrum, because they know that "this too shall pass." Once the child is calm, the parent can discuss the reasoning behind the tantrum and possible coping strategies for the next time they are emotionally triggered.

The LOVEE Method is also a form of self-care. Oftentimes, parents forget to care for themselves physically, mentally, and emotionally. Taking a moment to breathe and tend to their own challenging emotions is a way for parents to honor themselves. Practicing good self-care is also good parenting. When parents demonstrate how to take time for themselves and process their feelings in a healthy way, they serve as role models for their children to become well-adjusted and resilient in their own lives.

In Romantic Partnership

There are many beautiful things about being in partnership, but there are a lot of challenges, as well. When we get emotionally triggered by our partner, rather than say something we will regret, we can pause and practice the LOVEE Method, which allows us to *respond* to our partner from a rational and loving place, rather than a knee-jerk reaction.

The LOVEE Method shifts our brain activity from our amygdala to our prefrontal cortex (the site of reasoning). When we are reactive, we are operating from our amygdala and our habitual patterns from the past. Mindfulness adds the awareness that enables us to be less reactive and more present in our relationships.

The LOVEE Method also increases our emotional intelligence, meaning we become more aware of our own (and our partner's) habitual patterns. When we are more compassionate toward our own faults, we naturally become more compassionate toward our partner's shortcomings, as well.

The Equanimity practice is particularly helpful in that we can repeat the phrase: *They are who they are; may I accept them just as they are.* Accepting (rather than resisting) our partner's behavior allows the energy between the couple to flow fluidly.

Lastly, when we fill our own cups with self-compassion, and we meet our own emotional needs, we don't need to keep score. With daily practice of the LOVEE Method, we create a loving internal experience, therefore, we are not continually craving external validation from our partner. When we are sovereign in our ability to generate love and happiness from within, we are better able to share this overflowing love with our partner from a place of generosity rather than craving and expectation.

In Community

The LOVEE Method also helps to improve relationships with our friends. When we become more compassionate of our own thoughts and emotions, we naturally become more understanding when we see our friends behaving from their wounding.

With the Equanimity practice, we become less reactive and feel safer among our peers. The Value practice reminds us that we share the same joy as well as the same pain, and that we are all in this together. This acknowledgment of our shared humanity leads to feelings of empathy, connection, and community.

With Ourselves

The relationship with ourselves is the most important relationship of all. The LOVEE Method is ultimately a self-love practice since it creates a loving interaction between our awareness and our thoughts and emotions. This practice creates a safe container for challenging emotions (such as anger, anxiety, or depression) to be processed in a healthy way. The practice teaches us to embrace these emotions and give them the kindness and compassion they are calling out for, cultivating the very essence of self-love.

Due to neuroplasticity, a daily practice creates new neural pathways of compassion and equanimity. These qualities are reflected in our behavior and how we show up in the world. When we continually offer peace, love, and joy in our relationships, these qualities are often mirrored back to us. Ease and happiness start within, and these experiences are relational and cyclical.

With daily practice of the LOVEE Method, we empower ourselves since we are consciously choosing to create a beautiful internal experience, no matter how difficult our external circumstances may be. When we know how to create a loving and stable internal state, we can maintain balance when life's inevitable problems arise.

There Is Nothing to Fear

With the LOVEE Method, we no longer need to be afraid in life. We know that whatever painful experience arises, whether an external circumstance or an internal emotion, we have the tool to transform the pain into loving awareness. Since we know how to transform our suffering into love, we can see challenges as opportunities for growth and invitations to rise.

With less fear, we can be more optimistic and take greater risks because we know that we can handle problems when they occur. This tool provides the emotional resilience needed to cope with whatever life presents.

Even though we don't know what tomorrow will bring, we can rest easy since this practice serves as an emotional safety net. Having the LOVEE Method in our back pocket provides the ease and confidence needed to let our joy and curiosity—rather than our fear—take the lead in our lives.

The LOVEE Method Meditation

Practice whenever Anxiety, Anger, or Depression Arises

> Listen to the meditation online at:
> **www.meditationforbreastcancer.com**

Begin by gently closing your eyes or lowering your gaze to the floor. Take a moment to lift your spine and relax your shoulders, arms, and back. Allow your hands to rest wherever they are comfortable. Take a few deep breaths in and out through the nose. Allowing your body to soften, allowing your mind to settle.

Now I invite you to think about a situation in your life that is causing a difficult emotion within you, such as anger, anxiety or depression. Maybe it's related to your health, or perhaps it's a challenge with a co-worker, a family member, or a romantic partner. Rather than go into the story, shift your focus to the emotion that arises when you think about this difficult circumstance. If many emotions are present, I'd like you to choose just one emotion to work with for this exercise.

Let's begin with the Label practice. Start by focusing on the sensation of your breath at the chest, when you inhale the chest rises, when you exhale the chest falls. When you feel the emotion, bring your attention to it and give it a label, such as "Anger is rising," or "Fear is here," and then shift your focus back to the sensation of the breath at the chest. Continue with the Label practice. Continue to breathe.

Let's move to the Observe practice. Rather than resist or push away the emotion, we can relax and just observe it for what it actually is—an energy in motion. It comes and it goes. Just like a cloud drifting in the sky, we can observe our emotion rise to a peak, stay a little while, and then eventually fade away. If ever the emotion becomes too intense, you can always return to the pleasant sensation of the breath at your chest.

Now, try to locate the emotion as a sensation in the body. Scanning your body from head to toe, you may find the emotion has taken the form of tension in the shoulders, soreness in the back, or a rapid heartbeat. Bring your full attention to these bodily sensations, and bring a sense of curiosity to them. Continue to observe the sensations as they move and shift, expand and contract. If ever the sensations become too intense, you can always return your focus to the pleasant sensation of the breath at your chest.

Now let's move to the next letter, "V", which stands for value the emotion. Remind yourself this emotion is completely natural—feeling this way is simply part of the human journey. You are not alone in feeling this way. Others would feel this same emotion in this circumstance and we are all in this together. Valuing this emotion means that you value the entire spectrum of human emotions, and therefore valuing the entirety of this human experience and the preciousness of this beautiful life. Continue to take deep breaths and focus on the sensation of the breath at the chest area.

Now let's cultivate self-compassion with the Embrace practice. Bringing your hands in front of you in the shape of a cup, imagine that your emotion is in your hands. As if you are parenting yourself, bring your hands to your heart and embrace your emotion with tenderness and care. In your mind, say to the emotion, *I see you. I hear you. I've got you.*

Now, ask the emotion, *What do you need, sweetheart?* And then listen deeply and offer it what it needs, offering such phrases as: *You are always safe with me. I will never leave you. I respect you. I love you. I appreciate you. I will always be here for you.*

Say whatever words your emotion needs to hear to feel comforted, loved, and cherished. Savor the sweet feelings that come from offering yourself kindness and appreciation. Filling your body with your own love and compassion. Taking in a deep breath in and out through the nose, and allow your hands to gently release down to your lap.

Once you feel like your emotion has been soothed and cared for, we can move to the last letter of the LOVEE Method, "E" for equanimity, where we will accept the situation.

I invite you to bring your attention back to the situation that originally triggered the emotion. While thinking of this challenging circumstance, repeat one of these equanimity phrases. Choose the phrase that is most fitting to your circumstance:

Things are as they are; may I accept things just as they are.
He is who he is; may I accept him just as he is.
She is who she is; may I accept her just as she is.
I am who I am; may I accept myself just as I am.

Choose the phrase that is most fitting to your situation. Continue to breathe and repeat this phrase over and over again in your mind. Remembering that accepting something is not condoning it, or saying it's "okay" or "not okay", we are simply cultivating the quality of equanimity, a nonreactive mindset. Savoring the feeling of wellbeing that arises from full acceptance, full surrender to what *is*. Releasing all resistance and allowing whatever is here to be here.

If you're not feeling equanimity, that is also okay, just bring mindfulness to whatever you are experiencing and say, *May I hold this, too, with kindness.* If you are experiencing equanimity, allow the grounding and calming feelings to emanate throughout the body. Imagine yourself bringing this powerful essence of strength and grace to all of your life's circumstances.

Let's take three deep breaths to close the meditation. Bring one hand to your heart (where we cultivated compassion) and the other hand to your abdomen (where we cultivated equanimity). Inhale through the nose and exhale out the mouth. Inhale and exhale. Inhale and exhale. Begin to bring some gentle movement to the body, swaying your torso left and right. When you are ready, gently open your eyes.

Chapter 18

Moving Forward with a New Perspective

"One day she realized that unexpected things were always going to happen in life and the only control she had was how she chose to handle them. So, she made the decision to roll with the ups and downs with courage, humor, and grace. She was the queen of her own life and the choice was hers."
Kathy Kinney, comedian

A Time of Transition

I spent Christmas at Mom's house in Los Angeles. Although it was nice to spend the holidays with the family, I didn't feel grounded internally. I suddenly had a lot of time on my hands because I didn't have a job and the rigorous schedule of cancer treatment was over. And even though Will and I remained friends, we were no longer spending time together. So, I was left thinking, *What do I do now?*

All I knew was that I had more healing to do. This was still a very vulnerable time for me, not only physically, but also psychologically. This was the time to transition my identity from "cancer patient" back to a healthy person operating in the world. But I wasn't the same person I was before cancer. *Who am I now? How am I going to show up differently? How will I integrate the new me into my old life?*

I needed a quiet and safe place to sort through these psychological questions and stabilize my nervous system. Living in Venice Beach was hectic and not conducive for this experience. Luckily, a friend of mine had an open room starting in January in a large house nestled in the countryside of North County San Diego. Five other people lived there on a five-acre property near Palomar Mountain, along with five large fluffy wolf-dogs. Everyone in the house was kind, relaxed, and supportive of my vision of restoration. It was a beautiful place that was perfect for my healing process—*and for writing this book.*

With my housemates in North County San Diego, where I wrote this book.

In January, I moved into this peaceful home, and I started to get my physical strength back. I saw little sprouts of hair that felt like baby-bird feathers popping up all over my head. By the end of January, I had a proper pixie cut, my eyebrows were filling in and my eye-lashes had grown back. On an emotional level, the constant grip of anxiety began to loosen, and my nervous system was returning back to equilibrium.

Every three weeks, from January to May, I drove from San Diego to UCLA for a chemotherapy infusion. I had eleven of these treatments in total, and luckily the side effects were minuscule compared to the first six rounds. On February 14, I had minor surgery where Dr. Roostaeian surgically created a nipple for my new breast. Rather than receiving flowers or chocolate on Valentine's Day, I reclaimed my femininity.

My very last chemotherapy was on May 1, 2019. This date marked exactly one year and one day since that horrific phone call revealing my diagnosis on April 30, 2018.

On June 1, I received my nipple tattoo. The tattoo artist applied various shades of pink and beige to create a natural-looking areola. The size, shape, and color of my two breasts finally matched, and my journey as a breast cancer patient was officially over.

I took a pause. Although I was grateful to be alive and done with treatment, I felt profound sadness and compassion for the other women who didn't survive or would continue to struggle with breast cancer for the rest of their lives. I thought about their fear, since it was also my fear. I thought about their grief, since it was also my grief. This shared experience, along with a desire to serve, fueled my motivation to write this book in hopes that my story and these mindfulness practices could provide inspiration and ease in another woman's life.

The Camino

Even though Will would not be joining me, I decided to walk the Camino on my own—this trip was my victory lap, after all!

On the morning of October 1, 2019, I checked in at the Los Angeles International Airport for my flight to Madrid. I planned to walk the Camino for eight days, then explore Barcelona and Mallorca for a couple more weeks. It had been eleven months since my major surgery, and my body was finally strong enough to take on this physical endeavor.

One would think that I would be resentful since I had to postpone this trip—but I wasn't. Because of this year-long diversion with cancer, I would see the cathedrals in Barcelona with new eyes; I would swim the waters of Mallorca with a more thankful heart; I would walk the Camino de Santiago with more gratitude in every step.

Also, I would be walking the Camino on October 10, my 46th birthday. Fulfilling a life-long dream was the perfect way to celebrate my birthday and honor the precious gift of being alive—something I no longer took for granted.

Lessons Learned

After I boarded the plane, I sat back in my seat and lessons I'd learned this past year. I took out my journal, t__ page, and began to write:

What did I learn from this experience with cancer?

1. **Letting Go of Control.** I don't have control over what happens in life, but I *do* have control over how I react.
2. **The Importance of Positive Thinking**. My happiness is not determined by my circumstances, it is determined by my thoughts.
3. **Strength Through Surrender.** All suffering comes from resistance to a particular situation, not from the situation itself. When I don't resist, I don't suffer. So, rather than wishing things were different, I can surrender to whatever life presents me.
4. **Trusting Life.** Life is happening *for* me, not *to* me. I trust that whatever happens is what is best for my soul's evolution, even death. Death is a natural part of life and is no longer something to fear.
5. **The Importance of Self-Compassion.** Offering compassion toward myself transforms my suffering. Having a daily self-compassion practice creates a loving experience within, which allows me to be more understanding and compassionate with others.
6. **The Importance of Emotional Resilience.** Practicing the LOVEE Method cultivates equanimity and emotional resilience, which allow for a greater capacity for joy, compassion, and happiness.
7. **The Fragility of Life.** Life can be taken from us at any time, so I no longer take it for granted. Because life is so fragile and unpredictable, love and kindness are what really matters.
8. **Ego is an Illusion.** In seeing my mental and emotional patterns clearly, I realize that the ego doesn't exist—there is nothing to prove, seek, or defend. Rather than identify with my ego, I now identify with my Spirit—*my Spirit is who I am.*

Cancer hit the reset button in my life, and I was not turning back to my old ways of being. This experience gave me a new perspective on what was important in life. Probably the best thing that happened was that I became *more* myself because all of my inner nonsense fell away.

It was now time to integrate these lessons and establish how I would live my life moving forward. Although having cancer was intense, it was because of the severity of the circumstance that these eight truths were now fully embodied. From this complete dismantling of my psyche, I was able to build myself anew.

Honing the skills of mindfulness and emotional resilience throughout this journey did more than restore me to who I was before getting cancer; I had emerged from this experience transformed into a more authentic expression of who I was meant to be.

Landing in Spain

As the wheels of the plane touched down, I looked out the window, brimming with excitement about my upcoming adventure. I put on my backpack, stepped out of the plane, and took in a deep breath of Spanish air.

From the airport, I took a bus to the village of Triacastela—the starting place of my 100-mile trek to the city of Santiago de Compostela. I walked to the trailhead and looked up at the lush, winding, tree-lined trail. Before taking my first step on the path, I took a pause. I had eight days of walking ahead of me, but I knew I could do it.

Although I was walking by myself, I was not alone. I would be walking on the same trail that thousands of other pilgrims had trekked since the 9th century. I closed my eyes and imagined these pilgrims, risking their lives to accomplish this trek as an expression of their incredible devotion. I was filled with gratitude for the opportunity to be part of this inspiring slice of history, particularly since I was so close to not making it here.

Although I did not identify as Catholic, my faith in a higher power had deepened to a new level, and I was ready to embark on this journey as an act of reverence to the mystery. With each step of this walking meditation, I would say, "Thank you" to Spirit for protecting me, helping me overcome cancer, and allowing me to enjoy another day of this beautiful life.

Tears welled up in my eyes.

I made it, I thought with a smile. *I'm alive, and I'm here. I made it.*

Then, I took the first step …

Walking the Camino de Santiago, Spain.

Acknowledgements

First and foremost, I am grateful for my mom, Carolyn Marquez. She was with me for every appointment and every treatment. She was my rock and my angel. Thank you, Mom. I love you!

I also want to acknowledge my friends who offered support during my cancer treatment, as well as with producing this book: Aurora Rose, Sabrina Elizondo, Amanda Mince, Kirsten Morningstar, Nicole Goddard, Jenna Grayson, Kela Brousard, Bonnie Solomon, Maya Jabbur, Ceri Bethan Rose, Sally de Lourenco, Jason May, Jared May, Shannon Hayden, Shalini Serena Bahad, Liz Valadez, Ivy Glass, Brooke Benson, Barbara Jabbur, Lori Perkins, Betsy Finkelhoo, Riyaana Hartley, Denise Beaudoin, Nicole Doherty, Lisa Renta, Lauree Dash, David Kim, Curtis Baumgartner, Jordana Reim, Monica Frascona, Michelle Lapinski, Andrew Shepherd, Michelle Mackey, Nicole Polanco, Leif Cederblom, Tanya Rayvn, Dustin Valentine, Megan Pogoda, my cover designer Andrea Villafane, and my editor Marley Lynn of KN Literary Arts.

I also want to thank my medical team at UCLA Medical Center: Dr. Kelly McCann, Dr. Amy Kusske, Dr. Jason Roostaeian, Dr. Dennis Slamon, and my chemotherapy nurses Ruby Ortiz and Kelly LaMont. Thank you for dedicating your lives to saving ours. It was remarkable how hard this UCLA Health team worked for me, and always with such caring attitudes.

Lastly, I'd like to acknowledge my beloved meditation teachers: Heather Prete, Hilary Jackendoff, Chandresh Bhardwaj, Angelike Irene Dexter, Heidi Shaw, as well as Diana Winston, Marvin Belzer, and Julie Kosey from the UCLA Mindful Awareness Research Center (MARC).

To everyone named here, I am blessed to have you in my life. May the kindness you offered to me come back to you in spades. Thank you!

Jumping for joy as I reached the finish line of the Camino de Santiago!

Endnotes

Chapter 3

1. Matthew A. Killingsworth and Daniel T. Gilbert, "A Wandering Mind Is an Unhappy Mind," *Science* 330, no. 6006 (2010): 932, https://www.ncbi.nlm.nih.gov/pubmed/21071660.
2. Wendy Hasenkamp and Lawrence W. Barsalou, "Effects of Meditation Experience on Functional Connectivity of Distributed Brain Networks," *Frontiers in Human Neuroscience* 6 (2012): 38, https://www.ncbi.nlm.nih.gov/pmc/articles/PMC3290768/.
3. Debra A. Gusnard and Marcus E. Raichle, "A Default Mode of Brain Function," *Proceedings of the National Academy of Sciences* 98, no. 2 (2001): 676-682, https://doi.org/10.1073/pnas.98.2.676.
4. Veronique A. Taylor et al., "Impact of Meditation Training On the Default Mode Network During a Restful State," *Social Cognitive and Affective Neuroscience* 8, no. 1 (2013): 4-14, https://www.ncbi.nlm.nih.gov/pubmed/22446298.
5. Judson A. Brewer et al., "Meditation Experience is Associated with Differences in Default Mode Network Activity and Connectivity," *Proceedings of the National Academy of Sciences* 108, no. 50 (2011): 20254-20259, https://www.ncbi.nlm.nih.gov/pubmed/22114193.
6. Nerea Moreno and Agustin Gonzalez, "Evolution of the amygdaloid complex in vertebrates, with special reference to the anamnio-amniotic transition," *Journal of Anatomy* 211, no. 2 (2007): 151-163, https://www.ncbi.nlm.nih.gov/pmc/articles/PMC2375767/.

7   David Creswell et al., "Neural Correlates of Dispositional Mindfulness During Affect Labeling," *Psychosomatic Medicine* 69, no. 6 (2007): 560-565, https://www.ncbi.nlm.nih.gov/pubmed/17634566.

Chapter 6

1   David Creswell et al., "Neural Correlates of Dispositional Mindfulness During Affect Labeling," *Psychosomatic Medicine* 69, no. 6 (2007): 560-565, https://www.ncbi.nlm.nih.gov/pubmed/17634566.
2   G. Berlucchi and H. A. Buchtel, "Neuronal Plasticity: Historical Roots and Evolution of Meaning," *Experimental Brain Research* (2009): 307-319.
3   Britta K. Holzel et al., "Mindfulness practice leads to increases in regional brain gray matter density," *Psychiatry Research* 191, no. 1 (2011): 36-43, https://pubmed.ncbi.nlm.nih.gov/21071182.
4   David S. Black and George M. Slavich, "Mindfulness meditation and the immune system: a systematic review of randomized controlled trials," *Annals of the New York Academy of Sciences* 1373, no. 1 (2016): 13-24, https://www.ncbi.nlm.nih.gov/pmc/articles/PMC4940234/.
5   Linda Witek Janusek et al., "Mindfulness based stress reduction provides psychological benefit and restores immune function of women newly diagnosed with breast cancer: A randomized trial with active control," *Brain, Behavior, and Immunity* 80, no. 8 (2019): 358-373, https://pubmed.ncbi.nlm.nih.gov/30953776/.

Chapter 9

1   American Cancer Society (2018), https://www.cancer.org/research/cancer-facts-statistics/all-cancer-facts-figures/cancer-facts-figures-2018.html.
2   Helena Granstam Bjorneklett et al., "A randomised controlled trial of support group intervention after breast cancer treatment: results on anxiety and depression," *Acta Oncologica* 51, no. 2 (2012): 198-207, https://pubmed.ncbi.nlm.nih.gov/21923569/.

Chapter 12

1. Etymology Dictionary, https://www.etymonline.com/word/compassion.
2. Van der Kolk, Bessel. *The Body Keeps The Score: Brain, Mind, and Body in the Healing of Trauma*. New York, NY: Penguin Books, 2015.
3. Neff, Kristin. *Self-Compassion: The Proven Power of Being Kind to Yourself*. New York, NY: HarperCollins Books, 2011.
4. Neff, Kristin. https://self-compassion.org/the-physiology-of-self-compassion/.
5. Neff, Kristin. https://self-compassion.org/the-physiology-of-self-compassion/.

Chapter 15

1. Brach, Tara. *Radical Acceptance: Embracing Your Life with the Heart of the Buddha*. New York, NY: Bantam Books, 2003.
2. Chödrön, Pema. *Comfortable With Uncertainty: 108 Teachings on Cultivating Fearlessness and Compassion*. Boston, MA: Shambhala Publications, 2002.
3. Hanh, Thich Nhat. *Teachings on Love*. Berkeley, CA: Parallax Press, 2007.
4. Siegel, Daniel. *Mindsight: The New Science of Personal Transformation*. New York, NY: Bantam Books, 2011.
5. Treleaven, David. *Trauma-Sensitive Mindfulness: Practices for Safe and Transformative Healing*. New York, NY: W.W. Norton & Company, 2018.

Additional Resources

Chapter 6

Smalley, Susan and Winston, Diana. *Fully Present: The Science, Art, and Practice of Mindfulness.* Philadelphia, PA: Perseus Books, 2010.
Bolte-Taylor, Jill. *My Stroke of Insight: A Brain Scientist's Personal Journey.* New York, NY: Penguin Books, 2016.
Kabat-Zinn, Jon. *Wherever You Go There You Are: Mindfulness Meditation in Everyday Life.* New York, NY: Hachette Books, 1994.
Tolle, Eckhart. *The Power of Now: A Guide to Spiritual Enlightenment.* Vancouver, BC, Canada: Namaste Publishing, 1999.

Chapter 9

Brown, Brené. TED Talk 2012. *Listening to Shame.* https://www.ted.com/talks/brene_brown_listening_to_shame?language=en.
Hanh, Thich Nhat. *No Mud, No Lotus: The Art of Transforming Suffering.* Berkeley, CA: Parallax Press, 2014.

Chapter 12

Germer, Christopher. *The Mindful Path to Self-Compassion: Freeing Yourself from Destructive Thoughts and Emotions.* New York, NY: The Guilford Press, 2009.
Salzberg, Sharon. *Loving-Kindness: The Revolutionary Art of Happiness.* Boulder, CO: Shambhala, 1995.

Chapter 15

Hanson, Rick. *Hardwiring Happiness: The New Brian Science of Contentment, Calm, and Confidence.* New York, NY: Harmony Books, 2013.

Goleman, Daniel. *Emotional Intelligence: Why it can Matter More than IQ.* New York, NY: Bantam Books, 1995.

Chapter 17

Hanh, Thich Nhat. *Reconciliation: Healing the Inner Child.* Berkeley, CA: Parallax Press, 2010.

Printed in Great Britain
by Amazon